IMAGE AND IDEA IN
FIFTH-CENTURY GREECE

IMAGE AND IDEA IN FIFTH-CENTURY GREECE

Art and literature after the
Persian Wars

E.D. Francis

EDITED BY MICHAEL VICKERS

London and New York

First published 1990
by Routledge
11 New Fetter Lane, London EC4P 4EE

Simultaneously published in the USA and Canada
by Routledge
a division of Routledge, Chapman and Hall, Inc.
29 West 35th Street, New York, NY 10001

Typeset in 10/12pt Garamond by
Columns of Reading Ltd
Printed in Great Britain by
Biddles Ltd Guildford

British Library Cataloguing in Publication Data
Francis, E.D. (Eric David) 1940–1987
Image and idea in fifth-century Greece : art and
literature after the Persian Wars.
1. Greek arts. Ancient period.
I. Title   II. Vickers, Michael
700'.938

Library of Congress Cataloging in Publication Data
Francis, E.D. (Eric David), 1940–1987.
Image and idea in fifth-century Greece : art and literature after
the Persian wars / E.D. Francis: edited by Michael Vickers.
p.   cm.
Contains the Waynflete lectures, delivered under the auspices of
Magdalen College in 1983.
Includes bibliographical references.
1. Arts and society – Greece.   2. Allegories.   I. Vickers, Michael
J. II. Title.
NX180.S6F7   1990
700'.1'030949509015—dc20   89–49328

ISBN 0 415 01914 1

CONTENTS

NX
180
, S6F7
1990

ACKNOWLEDGEMENTS

We are grateful to the following for permission to reproduce illustrations:

Fig. 1: Hermitage Museum, Leningrad. *Fig. 2*: DAI, Tehran. *Fig. 3*: DAI, Rome. *Figs 4–5*: Chalcis Museum. *Fig. 7*: A.J. Spawforth. *Fig. 8*: after Furtwängler/Reichold. *Fig. 9*: Archaeological Museum, Naples. *Fig. 10*: DAI, Rome. *Fig. 11*: National Museums of Scotland. *Fig. 12*: Museum für Kunst und Gewerbe, Hamburg. *Figs 13–14*: after Furtwängler/Reichold. *Figs 15–17*: Antikenmuseum SMPK, Berlin. *Fig. 18*: Cabinet des Médailles, Paris. *Fig. 20*: after Furtwängler/Reichold. *Fig. 21*: Professor George Huxley. *Figs 22–4*: Metropolitan Museum, New York. *Fig. 25*: after Furtwängler/Reichold. *Fig. 26*: Museum of Fine Arts, Boston. *Figs 27–8*: after Furtwängler/Reichold. *Figs 29–30*: Ashmolean Museum, Oxford. *Fig. 31*: after Furtwängler/Reichold. *Figs 35–6*: after *Fouilles de Delphes*. *Figs 37–9*: after Ross 1855. *Fig. 40*: after Thompson and Wycherley.

FOREWORD

David Francis delivered the Waynflete Lectures in May 1983
during his tenure of the Waynflete Visiting Fellowship at
Magdalen College, Oxford. He always intended to enlarge the
lectures into a book along the lines of Simon Schama's *The
Embarrassment of Riches* or Robert L. Herbert's *Impressionism: Art,
Leisure and Parisian Society* (and there is still room for such a work),
but other research and teaching responsibilities as well as his
failing eyesight meant that large-scale revision was postponed. An
index of the effort he put into his classroom activities is that he
was awarded the University of Texas's Jean Holloway Award for
Teaching Excellence in Arts and Sciences and Regents' Faculty
Fellowship during this period. A partially edited version was found
among his papers after his death in March 1987, and this provided
the basis for this volume. The lectures are printed more or less as
they were given with the addition of notes. David's death is a great
loss to his friends, colleagues and students and his wide learning
and bravura performances will be greatly missed by all those who
knew and admired him and who benefited from his learning. His
knowledge of the Ancients' patterns of language and their modes of
thought, of classical literature and iconography was wholly exceptional, as many of his former students – and the editor – can attest.

Had David Francis lived to complete this work himself he would
have wished to thank in the first instance the President and Fellows
of Magdalen College, for providing intellectual stimulation,
creature comforts, and friendship. His time at Oxford was a very
happy one. In Texas, he would have thanked Professor Karl
Galinsky for encouragement and the University Research Institute
for financial support. Thanks are also due to the Wolfson
Foundation which generously supported the work which the author

ix

FOREWORD

and editor did together; to the Jowett Copyright Trustees and to Gilbert M. Denman Jr for financial support of the publication of these lectures; to Professor George Huxley for allowing the reproduction of the genealogical table; and to the following for providing photographs, and permission to publish them: the Antikenmuseum, Basel (Dr Margot Schmidt), Professor Gerold Walser of Basel, the Staatliche Museen, Berlin, Antikenmuseum (Dr Wolf-Dieter Heilmeyer and Dr Gertrud Platz), the Museum of Fine Arts, Boston (Dr John Herrmann), Professor A.D. Trendall of Bundoora, Victoria, the Museum of Chalcis (Dr E. Sakellarakis and Miss Amalia Carapaschalidou), the National Museums of Scotland, Edinburgh (Dr Elizabeth Goring), the Museo Archeologico, Naples (Dr Enrica Pozzi), the Metropolitan Museum of Art, New York (Dr Dietrich von Bothmer), Dr A.J. Spawforth of Newcastle-upon-Tyne, the Cabinet des Médailles, Bibliothèque Nationale, Paris (Mme H. Aghion), the German Archaeological Institute, Rome (Dr Martin Stadler), and the German Archaeological Institute, Tehran (Professor Peter Calmeyer). Thanks are also due to the Visitors of the Ashmolean Museum for granting the editor sabbatical leave in order to reconstruct these lectures.

This volume is dedicated to Deanne Francis, whose contribution to both its composition and publication cannot go unmentioned.

Michael Vickers

1

GREEK ART IN AN HISTORICAL SETTING

'Can it be that Athens' city still is undestroyed?' 'For so long as men live', the courier replies to Queen Atossa, 'Athens' defence is secure' (*herkos estin asphales*).[1] In this exchange Aeschylus' characters seem to echo language in which Apollo's priestess had earlier prophesied the survival of Athens, for when that city's representatives had come to supplicate the oracle, Aristonice declared 'in words than adamantine firmer: . . . may Zeus wide-seeing grant Athena that her wall of wood alone be undestroyed the which shall be of profit to you and to your children'.[2] Responding to these words Themistocles persuaded his fellow Athenians in the face of Persia's army to evacuate their city, man their newly-built fleet and entrust their fate to 'omnipotent Zeus, Athena Victory and Poseidon *asphaleios*, who forwards security'.[3] A decade before at Marathon, these same Athenians turned back from Attic soil the generals of Darius. Now at Artemisium and Salamis his son's navy was shattered by storms from the north, Themistocles' strategy and the favour of the gods. In the following year Xerxes' land army was no less decisively beaten at Plataea.

So when, at the beginning of the fifth century, Athenians had confronted the invading armies of Persia, they drove the stranger from their gate and sent the king in defeat and disarray back up the Royal Road to Susa. At once the victors celebrated this triumph in festival, art, and song, and, as Athens asserted a new hegemony by sea and land, her citizens alongside their allies pressed their advantage in order to liberate their Ionian kin and all the Greeks of Asia from the yoke of Persian rule. Victory, however, had not been easily won: in 480 Athens had indeed been sacked and her city twice occupied by Xerxes' army. Her citizens had watched helplessly from across the bay of Salamis as the smoke

1

rose from the fires of their pillaged sanctuaries. When these Athenians returned to rebuild their city, they transformed an alliance among states bent upon revenge into an empire which, in its turn, was to become no less an instrument of exploitation and repression. As a consequence, some Athenians at least began to reflect upon the nature of conquest and rule, and to reconsider the social and civic values their new power put at stake.

In the wake of victory Athenian politics was factionalized, but the son of Miltiades, strategist of Athens' victory at Marathon, soon and successfully seized the occasion to assert himself as Athens' leader. To Cimon, Joseph Wells has remarked, 'the humiliation of Persia was at least as important as the exaltation of Athens, in fact the two aims were with him largely identical'.[4] Like Alexander in the next century, Cimon was indeed a 'hammer of the Persians',[5] but his role in guiding Athenian policy at home as well as abroad in these years of post-war reconstruction and expansion was decisive for the future of his nation. 'It was the military genius and the diplomacy of Cimon which used the material and moral forces provided by Themistocles and Aristeides, and which won the conquests which Pericles organised only too thoroughly.'[6] Cimon or his political patrons chose Theseus as an heroic archetype for their policies since, unlike Heracles, Theseus' ancestry and mythical enterprise were pre-eminently Athenian. It may well be that local traditions already associated with him in Athenian folklore had not yet been formulated into an epic poem or indeed in any systematic programme. But whether or not the legends of Theseus had previously existed only in some disconnected form, it seems likely that they were now brought together, at times with significantly new variations, to support the propaganda of Cimon's career by expressing the image of a young leader, victorious by land and sea, at home and abroad. Theseus became, as it were, Cimon's signature – his *sphragis* – and the memories of Athenian triumph during the Persian wars from Marathon to Mycale, and his own double victory at the battle of the Eurymedon supplied recurrent subjects for contemporary art and song.

The Greeks had first come to know the Medes and the Persians when Cyrus moved west against the kingdoms of Phrygia and Croesus' Lydia in the middle of the previous century. As a consequence of Cyrus' victories, the eastern Greeks became subjects of the Great King and some of their artisans helped to build

Pasargadae, Susa and Darius' ceremonial palace at Persepolis.[7] Greeks of the Aegean and the mainland to its west thus gained the opportunity to grow familiar, at least by hearsay, with Persian customs and the grandeur associated with the court of the Achaemenid monarch, and this experience came at a time when most Greek states, and Athens among them, were in the throes of rebellion or had already abolished the rule of tyrants in preference for more democratic forms of government.

The Greek attitude towards outsiders was a complex one: they referred to all who could not speak their language as 'barbarian', and frequently attributed demeaning ethical stereotypes to those who lived beyond the Hellenic pale. At the same time, the Greeks recognized some hereditary relationship with the peoples of the east. The eponymous ancestors of the Medes and Persians – Perses and Medus – were both sons of Greek heroes, albeit sired of exotic women, one of whom, though oriental herself, could nonetheless claim Corinthian descent. Zeus' first human son became lord of Egypt and those who returned to Greece to found the great cities of Argos and Thebes were his descendants. When Argive Diomedes met Glaucus at Troy, the Lycian warrior was able to assert his own Corinthian ancestry traced from Bellerophon who had himself once come east to fight the chimaera. As Greeks in the fifth century sought paradigms from their own mythology to express their experience of the oriental as an enemy of Hellenic order, an exemplar of ethical confusion, they found parallels in the generation of giants who had opposed Zeus' attempt to establish his new Olympian government; in physiological hybrids like the chimaera, constructed of male parts, but once compounded, *Giftmädchen* to national security; and likewise in the tribe of Amazons, an army of barbarous viragos doomed as women to succumb to the sword of the Greek soldier; and so the Trojan War itself came to provide a popular analogue for recent historical events.[8]

In the fifth century the Persians represented the 'barbarian' *par excellence* and an Athenian was characteristically taught to disdain those habits of luxury that had rendered the mighty kingdom of Darius and Xerxes an adversary whom the Greeks against all odds had successfully vanquished. They had reason to feel confident that they could repel the invader from without, but the real dangers to their survival lay inside their own communities as the Thebes of Sophocles' Oedipus or Euripides' Dionysus was to discover to her cost. Persian behaviour, as an image of the exotic, though at times it might attract could also provide a paradigm of what to avoid. As Persia's kings, like Xerxes on Aeschylus' stage, became models of despotism whose inherent weakness must inevitably bring about their collapse, so Athens' leaders sought to define their own political identity by reference to the enterprise of those who in myth and act had punished such arrogance and guaranteed liberty for their countrymen.

It is the reflection of ideas such as these in Greek (and particularly, but by no means synonymously, Athenian) art, poetry, and public buildings during the generation following Xerxes' retreat which I wish to discuss today in these lectures. Towards the end of the fifth century, with Sparta closing in by land and concluding an alliance with Persia,[9] the Milesian poet Timotheus used the occasion of Athens' renewed success at sea to celebrate her enemies' defeat at Salamis some seventy years before.[10] Seeing the outcome of that battle from his throne above the bay, Xerxes calls out to his attendants:

> Come, no delay,
> Yoke my four-horse chariot,
> Bring my countless wealth
> To the wagons and burn the tents:
> May none of them profit from my treasure.[11]

But against the monarch's wish, Greece did indeed 'profit from his treasure', and Herodotus describes the victors of Plataea as they gazed upon the wealth of 'many tents richly adorned with furniture of gold and silver, gilded and silver-plated couches, golden bowls, mixing vessels, and drinking-cups . . . bracelets, torques, and daggers of gold',[12] and in particular Xerxes' war-tent left in the care of his field general, Mardonius, in which Pausanias, the Greek commander-in-chief, amazed at its opulence, ordered the cooks and bakers to prepare a Persian feast.[13] There is no need to recall in detail the inventories of these spoils divided up among the victors to be dedicated at both their pan-Hellenic and civic sanctuaries,[14] but I select three examples from the artefacts of Greek private and public life upon which Persian antecedents may have exercized their influence.

First, the development of Greek drinking vessels known as rhyta has been much discussed in terms of Persian prototypes (Fig. 1)[15] and even if East Greek intermediaries played a part in the early history of this vase-shape,[16] the increasing popularity of these vessels is likely to reflect Athenian acquaintance with the spoils of victory. Second, there can be little doubt, in view of Hubertus von Gall's recent demonstration, that Pericles' music hall, the Athenian Odeion, was constructed under the influence of Achaemenid architecture,[17] and Plutarch may well have been correct in reporting that the tent of Xerxes I have just mentioned provided its specific model.[18] Von Gall accordingly draws attention to Broneer's tempting if controversial thesis that, in the 470s, this tent actually entered service at Athens as the scene (Gk. *skene*) for the temporary theatre of Dionysus.[19] Imagine the spectacular effect that Aeschylus may have achieved in 472 if he presented Atossa, Darius, and the whole court of Susa, with Xerxes paraded in desolation and defeat before an audience of triumphant Athenians, and telling the news of his astounding humiliation in what had lately been a pre-eminent symbol of his own majesty. Again, one may wonder if the conical roof of the Athenian Tholos, known as 'Skias', the 'parasol', reflects more than merely the technical invention of a skilful architect. Dorothy Thompson has noted the resemblance between the design of this building and the round, pointed tents which the Persians used on campaign,[20] but a parasol itself may provide an even more relevant point of departure. Not only was the parasol regarded as a foppish conceit, asiatically bizarre,[21] but we can see Achaemenid kings themselves portrayed in procession or upon their thrones protected by such sunshades (Fig. 2).[22] I shall presently return to the building programme of which the Tholos in the Athenian Agora seems to have been a part, but for the moment it is enough to recall P.J. Rhodes' hypothesis that the Tholos may have been constructed after Ephialtes' death to house the presidents of Athens' council, newly established according to the constitutional reforms associated with his name.[23] In these terms the function of the parasol has been fundamentally recast. No longer does it shade an oriental and hereditary despot from the sun, but instead houses the temporary leaders of a democratically elected government of the free.

I have undertaken to present some aspects of fifth-century Athenian art in an historical setting and shall choose two monuments which may illustrate both the point and the difficulty of such an undertaking. Many practical obstacles indeed confront this enquiry, not least those derived from fundamental questions of principle. Let me summarize some of these obstacles at once and I shall return in due course to each of them in more detail. While much may be known of the military, political and social history of Athens during the first half of the fifth century, no one will deny that the historian of this period swiftly moves beyond securely ascertainable fact to the reconstruction of events and political movements whose record is often at best ambiguous. In interpreting Greek art and poetry as, in some sense, occasional, one would prefer to be more precisely certain than is usually possible at this period about not only the character, but indeed the date of the occasion being celebrated. Even the qualified assertion that poetry and art in the early fifth century may allude to any specific occasion is likely in some quarters to arouse suspicion, for many hold to the view that Greek art and literature conform to their own independent and autonomous conventions and that to consider their imagery in terms of some topical reference represents an ignorant and fruitless attempt to vandalize their integrity.

I shall not discuss literary issues in this chapter, but rather Greek material culture whose students have often been hesitant, especially in minor arts like vase-painting, to interpret mythical scenes in a topical sense, preferring instead to analyse stylistic relations both of the decoration and of the proportions of the building or vessel that include it. 'An influential school of thought', so Andrew Stewart tells us, 'holds that the evolution of Greek art is so logical, undeviating and regular as to leave no room for the operation of social factors upon it'. Stewart takes particular issue with the attitude he attributes by way of example to Rhys Carpenter and which he describes as the 'exaltation of the formal imperative to the status of a universal law . . . buttressed by a curiously mechanistic . . . psychology that attempts to reduce all sensory experience to simple physiological processes in the eye of the observer'. [24] The vision of such an eye, trained to observing Wölfflin's *Prinzipien*, is likely also to systematize the objects of its gaze through the lens of yet another principle, the 'principle of continuous evolution'. This is no casual use of the term 'evolution'. The principle entered the study of Greek art in the nineteenth century as the deliberate offspring of Darwinian gradualism. What was newly deemed valid in the work of nature, not least geological nature, was extended to the explanation of the material culture of antiquity. While Percy Gardner was not the first to draw this analogy, he does so with disarming frankness:

6

there is not in the whole history of art any so regular and
gradual progress to be observed as in Greek sculpture. . . .
The whole process is an evolution which may be compared for
regularity and order with the geological evolution of the
earth. It is precisely this rule of law which makes the study of
Greek art so excellent a training in historic research.[25]

How, one may wonder, can it be 'so excellent a training' if such a
state of affairs is without parallel 'in the whole history of art'? And
as 'a training in historic research'? The enterprise Gardner outlines
has nothing to do with human history. His concern is to
reconstruct typological change, but the measure of its supposedly
steady march need not be directly calibrated with the progress of
historical time.

By now I have mentioned problems arising from both the
historical record and prevailing attitudes towards the material of
the study I have proposed to undertake. Moreover, the dates of the
evidence I wish to discuss are often far from certain. In discussing
the Athenian Treasury at Delphi John Boardman notes 'the lack of
absolute dates for works of sculpture' at the time of its
construction[26] and goes on to point out

the difficulty of comparison with Attic vase-paintings whose
sequences may be well established but whose absolute dates
are little more secure than those for sculpture. Moreover this
is a period in which the draughtsman may lead the sculptor
in introducing anatomical innovations, and close
correspondence may not have been achieved in features which
are our main stylistic criteria for date. And there is always
the problem presented by the possibilities of avant-garde
work by a young artist or conservative work by an old
artist.[27]

Small wonder that 'students of Greek art', as Stewart suggests, 'are
suspicious of attempts to explore the social dimensions of their
subject. In a discipline where hard facts are at a premium, a
reluctance to pile what may be wild surmise on what is often
already shaky conjecture seems perfectly justifiable'.[28] Well then,
are we to conclude that someone who seeks to find Athenian art
within its historical setting must instead discover himself as a
Pyrrhonist in that condition of *epokhe* which Sextus Empiricus
defines as 'a standstill of the intellect, as a result of which we

neither deny nor affirm anything'?[29] Instead, let us look at some *signa priscae artis* in their architectural context and consider the 'shaky conjectures' on which our present understanding of them rests and judge for yourselves how wild is our surmise about their character and intent, and about the events which may have occasioned their creation.

In 198 BC Lucius Flamininus and Attalus, king of Pergamum, laid siege to the Euboean city of Eretria. Livy, reporting this event, writes of the massive bombardment inflicted upon the city to which the defenders finally succumbed, despite great bravery. Surveying their booty the captors found remarkably little gold and silver bullion, but a wealth of art 'disproportionate to the size of the city and its other resources'. Livy describes these treasures as *signa tabulae artis ornamenta eius generis*, 'statues of ancient art', *ars prisca*. As a Latin counterpart of Greek *arkhaios*, *priscus* could appropriately characterize early Greek sculpture seen through Roman eyes without, of course, implying anything of the modern, technical use of the term 'archaic' to refer to a period of early Greek art. Eretria's conquerors were interested in plunder, and Livy notes the Roman fleet standing offshore, laden with Euboean spoils. On the first day of his triumph at Rome, four years later, Titus Flamininus displayed among the loot from his eastern campaigns *signa . . . marmorea*, the first occasion on which 'marble sculpture' is reported to have been seen in that city. One *signum . . . marmoreum* (Fig. 3),[30] found in the Villa Ludovisi, may well have taken part in Flamininus' triumph. After all, from an ideological standpoint, a captured Amazon archer represents a just subject for a general to present before his fellow citizens on his return from eastern conquest. But enough of 'wild surmise' for we know that this Amazon came originally from the same pediment which contained the Athena in Figure 4 and the well-known group of Theseus and Antiope, the Amazon queen in Figure 5,[31] and we know that the pediment adorned the temple of Apollo Daphnephorus, Eretria's chief shrine.

Martin Robertson thinks it 'odd to find this particularly Attic theme so lavishly displayed on a great temple in another city',[32] though I expect he would agree that the Eretrians themselves are likely to have understood why it was there. As James Redfield puts it, 'To understand any story is to participate imaginatively in the culture of its intended audience.'[33] But before we can judge how an Amazonomachy including Theseus and Athena might be considered a decoration suitable to an Eretrian gable, we must know something of the circumstances of the temple's erection. The distinguished team of Swiss archaeologists who recently looked into this question decided, on grounds of architectural style, that construction had begun *c.* 530, but, again on stylistic grounds, that the pedimental sculpture dates from some 25 years later. Most scholars prefer a slightly earlier date, *c.* 510, for the sculpture, but Professor Boardman has recently asked: 'Could the temple be later than 490 BC?'[34] 490 was a critical year in the city's history and it is as close to certain as such things can be that whatever temple served Apollo's Eretrian cult in that year was destroyed by fire. Therefore even the possibility implicit in John Boardman's question introduces a discrepancy of no less than forty years among recent attempts to judge the temple's construction date[35] and, though it is but one instance, so substantial a discrepancy discourages confidence in the security of a chronological scale derived from purely stylistic criteria as a means of dating pre-classical Greek art with precision.

'Could the temple be later than 490 BC?' At the beginning of the fifth century when Miletus spurred Ionia to revolt against her Persian overlords, Eretria and Athens – alone among Greek states west of the Aegean – answered Aristagoras' appeal to contribute to the Ionian cause. Eretria's decision to join the expedition was apparently not based on any Athenian alliance, but repaid the Milesians for past military assistance. So Eretria sent five warships to escort Athens' squadron of twenty transports, the ships Herodotus describes as *arkhe kakon*, the 'beginning of evils for Greeks and barbarians'.[36] Persian reprisals show that Darius judged Eretria to have been fully implicated in the Ionian revolt so that when his generals came to exact vengeance on the Athenians in 490, before crossing to the mainland at Marathon, they landed first on Euboea to punish the Eretrians. 'No sooner had they entered the city walls', so Herodotus tells us, 'than they plundered and burnt the temples (*ta hira*) in the town in revenge for the burning of their own temples at Sardis'.[37] Considering the major importance of Apollo's cult at Eretria, we cannot doubt that his shrine was among those destroyed during the Persian attack.

When Kourouniotis first excavated the temple site in the 1890s, he identified traces of two successive structures, one wooden, the other made of marble.[38] He dated the wooden temple to the sixth century and the marble one to the first half of the fifth.

Kourouniotis was influenced by stylistic arguments which seemed to favour a sixth-century date for the pedimental sculpture and so concluded that the marble figures of Athena, Theseus and Antiope came from the wooden temple. When a team of Swiss archaeologists re-examined the site in the 1960s, they saw traces of even earlier foundations, but discovered no stratigraphic evidence sufficient to revise the building sequence Kourouniotis had reconstructed. Moreover, they confirmed Kourouniotis' judgement that the marble temple showed no signs of reconstruction and had no successors. On the other hand, they substantially revised Kourouniotis' view of the date of the two buildings. Auberson now dated the wooden temple as early as 670 and, as I have mentioned, thought that construction had begun on its marble successor *c.* 530 or soon thereafter.[39] He therefore believed that this marble temple was the one the Persians destroyed. According to Auberson, 'there is not a single architectural element, not even a block which allows for the possibility of reconstruction during the fifth or fourth centuries.' I accept the consequences of this important observation that the marble temple which is in any case generally agreed to have been the last temple on the site, at no time in its history underwent significant reconstruction (or replacement by some more modest, substitute structure). On the other hand, we may question the chronological significance which Auberson attaches to his stylistic criteria. Perhaps the architectural elements which Auberson has confidently dated to the same decade as the Siphnian Treasury in fact belong to the next century. In his recent analysis of the proportions of Doric capitals, J.J. Coulton classifies evidence from the Eretrian Temple in the same group as the temple of Zeus at Olympia; he does not therefore conclude that the buildings were contemporary.[40]

Although Kourouniotis' decision to attribute the pedimental sculptures to the sixth century was based on his judgement of their style, it was evidence of a very different kind which persuaded him that the cult of Apollo continued to flourish at Eretria even after the Persian attack. Inscriptions dating from the fourth century and later refer to dedications made 'within the *hieron* of Apollo Daphnephorus' or (if Kourouniotis' supplement is credible) 'before his *naos*'. Are we to believe that the 'shrine' in question was no more than a figment of folk memory, a pile of rubble or, at most, a burnt-out shell, *Perserschutt*, at which Eretrian devotees of Apollo piously continued to gather and to make substantial offerings two centuries after its premature destruction?[41] The scene is a possible one, though hardly compelling. Moreover, all the inscriptions whose findspots we know were excavated within the temenos of the temple. After all, it is these inscriptions which supply the basic evidence for identifying the temple's cult and the god's title. They also provide a kind of documentation which, I submit, testifies to the temple's history in a far more telling manner than Auberson's faith in the detailed correlation of style with historical time that led him to dismiss the possibility of a post-Marathonian date.

Having asserted my hypothesis with some vehemence, I would be less than candid not to draw attention to a consideration which robs it of certainty. The inscriptions speak only of 'the *hieron*', a term which can refer to a place of cult not necessarily commemorated by the presence of a temple. Some might therefore even prefer to take these epigraphic data as evidence against the post-Marathonian existence of Apollo's temple at Eretria.[42] On the other hand, *hieron* was used both by Herodotus[43] and in Ionic inscriptions to designate an actual building; it was of course 'the temples' (*ta hira*), not 'the cults' of Eretria which, according to Herodotus, the Persians 'burnt' (*enepresan*) in 490. Moreover, despite Herodotus' report of the burning of Eretria's *hira* the marble temple has so far yielded no evidence of damage (let alone destruction) by fire. The epigraphic evidence therefore does not prove beyond doubt that the marble temple is 'later than 490', but it certainly allows such a possibility, the implications of which deserve attention. For example, since Auberson has demonstrated that the marble sculpture belonged to the marble temple, not to its wooden predecessor, the pedimental Amazonomachy should in that case also be considered in a post-Marathonian context.[44]

But how long after the battle of Marathon, on this hypothesis, might Eretria's marble temple have been built? At this point, our evidence becomes even less straightforward. If we accept the so-called Oath of Plataea with its injunction against the restoration of temples burnt or otherwise destroyed by the Persians as the authentic reflection of an oath sworn in 479 and universally enforced, then we might prefer to date the temple's construction to the decade prior to the battle of Plataea. While I know of no evidence which excludes the possibility that the temple was at least substantially under way by the time the Persians returned to Greece, there are also other factors to be weighed. We know next to nothing about the extent to which Eretria's population and its material resources survived the Persian assault or what share she may have had in the spoils of war. Although Herodotus tells us that her people were enslaved in accordance with Darius' orders and deported to a settlement in the Euphrates valley near the bitumen wells outside Susa,[45] many must have escaped this fate since Eretria contributed galleys to the Greek fleet at Artemisium and Salamis,[46] and joined the Styreans in sending a small detachment of hoplites to fight at Plataea.[47] The Eretrians' name was entered on the Serpent Column at Delphi and it seems unnecessary to invoke chicanery as an explanation for their presence.[48] Despite her apparent omission from the pan-Hellenic dedication at Olympia, Eretria herself dedicated in that sanctuary a large, bronze bull,[49] perhaps in part as a complement to Athens and an allusion to her own involvement in the first, Marathonian campaign. We read of modest tribute quotas assessed against Eretria later in the century,[50] but there are too many unknown factors which make it hazardous to correlate recorded tribute figures with judgements about the actual wealth of a community under Athenian taxation. In any case, socio-economic hypotheses of this kind have no bearing on the date of the temple's construction. They merely suggest, as does the epigraphic evidence I have already mentioned, that a community continued to exist at Eretria after the Persian Wars, a community which at any rate in 198 BC was substantial enough to attract Flamininus' attention and, for a time, to withstand his forces.

Who built the temple? Again, we do not know, but the cooperation of Athens and Eretria in their commando raid on Sardis and their shared experience as the targets of Darius' campaign of reprisal are factors likely to have fostered a special relationship between these two cities. Eretria, Sir John Myres reminds us, 'was more than a normal city-state. Like Athens in Attica, it was the metropolis of all south Euboea except Carystus and Styra'.[51] And, as Myres also observes, 'it was part of the exceptional fortune of Athens to be the residuary heir of two great precursors, Eretria and Miletus, both devastated by the Persians.' John Boardman's description of the pedimental sculpture as 'comfortably rounded in a non-Athenian manner'[52] does not contradict the possibility that Eretria received material assistance from her increasingly powerful neighbour. Indeed, Professor Boardman himself thinks that the choice of subject was 'clearly inspired by Athens'.[53] Athens' interest in appropriating for herself the mantle of Eretria's former seapower would be understandable enough, and it is no less reasonable to suppose that the city which, only a short time before the Sardis venture, had reduced and colonized the territory of Chalcis, Eretria's ancient rival to the north, now sought to extend her influence throughout the whole island of Euboea. From motives such as these, Athens might well have come to her ally's aid and helped her to rebuild her shattered shrine. The restoration of Eretria's ancient temple to Apollo, whose local cult emphasized *daphnephoria* with its Delphic associations, could provide a suitable and pious act of thanksgiving for the deliverance of both communities from barbarian aggression. But when was the temple built? A date in the 480s allows a relative chronology which takes the Oath of Plataea into full account, but, while we know little enough of Athenian politics during that decade, we have nothing on events at Eretria; her own historians are lost and A.W. Gomme rightly objects that Herodotus' account of the fate of her citizens is 'not altogether an acceptable story, as it is told'.[54] On the other hand, while Herodotus reports in another context that the Euboeans 'had taken no precautions against the threat of war',[55] we may wonder if Eretria would have been able to rebuild her temple without outside help and whether Athenian resources would have been expended on temple reconstruction in another city, rather than on preparing their own defences against the storm brewing in the east. As a time of consolidation and expansion in the wake of more decisive victories, the 470s might seem to offer a more favourable historical context for so substantial an undertaking.

Can the iconography provide any clue? We would be better able to answer this question if the sculptural remains were not so fragmentary. So far as we know, nothing remains of the front gable, but since we have traces of a roof it is reasonable to suppose that one existed and that, like the west pediment, it was decorated.[56] We might guess that Apollo dominated the front gable, but perhaps it was Athena as at Aegina, and in the context of what action we do not know. The Swiss archaeologists' decision to date the sculpture of the rear gable *c.* 505 was related to historical considerations: citing the adoption of democratic constitutions by both cities at the end of the sixth century, Auberson and Schefold somewhat lamely suggest that the imagery of the extant pedimental sculpture represents a compliment to her Athenian alliance.[57] It should be said, however, that we know

13

rather less than this statement implies about the attitude of Eretria's leaders towards Athens at this period. Though Eretria may, for reasons of self-interest, have supported Athens in 506 in her war against Chalcis, it was obligation to Miletus, not alliance with Athens which, according to Herodotus, caused Eretria to take part in the Ionian revolt. Accepting an earlier date for the sculpture, Werner Gauer argues that the theme anticipates the joint role of Athens and Eretria in attempting to deliver their Ionian kin from Persian domination.[58] This hypothetical 'complement to their seers' seems to me a little far-fetched and we are warned of the subjective character of iconographic interpretation. On the other hand, the chief subject of the Amazonomachy, Theseus' abduction of Antiope, can be accepted – as it has been in other contexts – as a fitting, mythical template for the rape of Sardis.[59] With Eretrian Apollo perhaps on the east pediment and Athens' goddess dominating the rear, we can readily envisage a powerful image of the participation of these two states in the Ionian revolt, regardless of the reverse which forced their retreat. The iconography of the temple's decoration which includes acroterial victories accords well with the post-Marathonian date which the archaeological evidence allows.

While I fully acknowledge the possibility that the temple predates 480, let me mention some of the considerations that might weigh in favour of a date in the 470s. All these considerations assume some Athenian involvement in the building programme. In 490 the Persians had used Carystus, 'an Eretrian outpost'[60] on the southern tip of Euboea, as a base for their operations against Eretria and Athens.[61] Ten years later, Carystus sent ships to the Persian navy at Salamis[62] and, following the battle, only with great reluctance provided the financial contribution to the Greek fleet demanded by Themistocles.[63] In retaliation for this 'tarnished record' and in order to coerce her to join the new alliance, 'the Athenians', so Thucydides reports, 'made war upon Carystus',[64] thereby bringing Euboea fully under their control. The rebuilding of Apollo's temple at Eretria can perhaps be seen as a peaceful counterpart of this imperial enterprise. Moreover, we know how important the theme of Theseus became in Athenian, and particularly, Cimonian, political propaganda during the 470s. How early and in what form his legends developed, it will be part of the purpose of future lectures to assess. A final point: John Boardman has drawn attention to the prominence of the *gorgoneion* on Athena's aegis, recalling 'the earlier role of gorgons at pediment centres'.[65] While this *gorgoneion* may in general terms have retained its conventional, apotropaic reference, it is tempting in view of its iconographic context, to associate it with the Athenian intention, formed in the aftermath of the Persian defeats at Salamis, Plataea and Mycale, of transforming *phobos*, 'fear', from themselves to their Persian adversary who had for so long inspired that emotion among the Greeks.[66] In the Amazonomachy of Apollo's Eretrian temple, the divinity of Athens presides over her new protégé's triumph against the mythical counterpart of the common aggressor of Eretria and Athens. Eretria thus advertises on her temple the aegis of her great ally and, if the time is ripe, the *sphragis* of Athens' new leader, Cimon. From this standpoint, it is no longer 'odd to find this particularly Attic theme so lavishly displayed on a great temple in another city'.

In her influential study of archaic Greek sculpture, Brunilde Ridgway writes that 'in Eretria the Persian attack of 490 . . . gives a *terminus ante quem* for the pedimental sculpture of Apollo Daphnephoros'.[67] On the contrary, the Persian attack may well provide the temple's *terminus post quem*. In this connection it is therefore interesting to note that Ridgway is puzzled by several stylistic features which she believes would favour a post-sixth-century date were it not that the sculpture 'should precede the Persian destruction in 490'.[68] Professor Ridgway, to quote A.W. Verrall on a different enigma, has 'put a statue upon its head, and then complained of the statuary for representing a man with his feet in the air'.

Pausanias does not mention the ruins of Apollo's temple at Eretria, but he does report, for example, that the Athenian Treasury at Delphi was built from the spoils of Marathon, that is, after 490 BC.[69] Apart from the French excavators of this Treasury, however, very few scholars nowadays would countenance such a view. As John Boardman remarks, 'it is a measure of the confidence of scholars in their chronology for archaic Greek art that they are ready to set aside [Pausanias'] testimony and prefer an earlier date'.[70] It is no less a measure of their confidence in stylistic dating that they can assign Eretria's temple of Apollo to the sixth century, usually without even mentioning the epigraphic evidence which at least allows a date in the fifth.

T.J. Dunbabin once wrote that 'all the accepted system of dates, Greek and Italian, historical and archaeological, is interdependent, and when part of the series moves all must move.'[71] I see Dunbabin's point, but our evidence speaks against its validity, except in somewhat global terms which are themselves defined by a close reading of individual cases of the kind I have just discussed. Let me illustrate the problem by reference to a well-known example. I mentioned that Auberson assigns the architecture of the Eretrian temple to the same decade as the Siphnian Treasury at Delphi. Does the Siphnian Treasury therefore also postdate Marathon? Not necessarily, since Herodotus unambiguously implies that the Treasury had been recently dedicated at the time of the Samian attack upon Siphnos c. 525.[72] Critics at home and abroad have dismissed any chronological revision of the Eretrian evidence which runs counter to preconceptions based on style by declaring that Herodotus must have misreported the Persian attack upon Eretria's temples. One might retort with equal justice (and disregard for documentary sources) that Herodotus was mistaken when he gave us our *terminus ante quem* for the Siphnian Treasury since Herodotus provides the only direct testimony for what is generally regarded as 'our best fixed point in all the history of archaic art'.[73] For the time being, I would prefer to accept an element of uncertainty in our understanding of the chronology of pre-classical Greek art and to follow the evidence where it leads, even when the conclusions it implies may, on currently prevailing criteria, seem contradictory.

To close this first chapter I have chosen another example which involves a cult, but this time the building is in Athens. Important chronological issues are again relevant, but I am primarily concerned with the building's function and its relation to the structures adjacent to it. While the building, so far as we know, was not decorated, it clearly illustrates the importance of considering historical and social factors when defining the original use of an excavated structure. In this case, the issues range from the history of Athenian religion and of the administration of the city government to that of literacy in fifth-century Greece.

In the conflagration which engulfed Sardis at the outbreak of the Ionian revolt Herodotus singles out the destruction of 'the temple of Cybele, a goddess worshipped in that part of the world'. According to Herodotus, 'the Persians later made this the pretext for burning the temples of Greece'.[74] In his recreation of the battle of Salamis, Timotheus portrays two scenes from the prison-house of doomed men, stranded on the island of Psyttaleia[75] from which, as Aeschylus and Herodotus both tell us, no Persian escaped alive.[76] In the first we hear a group, abandoned and naked on the beach, calling upon their native lands, the tree-crowned vales of Mysia and their homes in Sardis which they will never see again (Timotheus, *Persians* lines 98–118). The call to their homeland goes unanswered (lines 119–20) and they look to another source of aid, the mother goddess of their mountains, Cybele (lines 121–6). The marooned sailors invoke their 'divine mother', but again to no avail. For these men there will be no homecoming and we leave Timotheus as he abandons them, bewailing their fate (139).

In mainland Greece Pindar sings of fostering the cult of the Mountain Mother and Pan apparently at Thebes,[77] but when and how was the cult of the Asiatic Mother of the Gods introduced to Athens? The question is not a trivial one since that divinity has such patently oriental connections that we should try to understand the nature of her liturgical presence at Athens. And so we turn to Martin Nilsson's monumental history of Greek religion. Nilsson cites a story that during a time of plague, the Athenians consulted Delphi to learn the cause of their misfortune. The oracle reminded them that they had once maltreated a mendicant priest of the Great Mother of Phrygia whom they should therefore propitiate. And so the Athenians built her a temple and introduced the practice of her cult. And when did this take place? At the end of the sixth century.[78] How did Nilsson know that? Because while Nilsson was writing his history, American archaeologists thought that they had actually discovered the temple of the Mother right there in the Athenian Agora and dated it to the early years of the democracy.[79] No matter that otherwise we hear nothing of the Mother from Athenian sources until the 420s, the decade, perhaps not coincidentally, following a plague worthy of doxographers, and it is to the social chaos of the Peloponnesian War which saw the arrival in Athens of so many exotic cults, religions of emergency, that E.R. Dodds plausibly attributes the Mother's advent.[80] By that time, however, according to Homer Thompson and his colleagues, her original temple, the 'archaic Metroon', had long ago disappeared, a casualty of the Persian sack.[81]

The building lay in the southwest corner of the Agora, south of a small temple of Apollo Patroos, a cult with Ionian overtones, and north of the Old Council Chamber, the Old Bouleuterion. The Tholos was constructed on the south side of the Old Bouleuterion in order to accommodate the *prytaneis*, the presidents of the council for whom, before the period of Ephialtes' reforms, no undisputed evidence exists.[82] The excavators give us clear information about the stratigraphic relationship of these various structures. The Great Drain was constructed before the Tholos, and the two buildings to its north. Both of these buildings, however, belong to the same building programme as the Great Drain, and they are directly aligned on it. The building to the north of the Old Council Chamber, the so-called Temple of the Mother, was built slightly later than the Bouleuterion to which it is adjoined by means of a retaining wall. The criteria for dating this building are therefore the same as those governing the Council Chamber, so what is the date of the Council Chamber? The excavators originally dated it *c.* 500 to the early years of Cleisthenic democracy,[83] but Homer Thompson has recently drawn public attention to the fire-damaged blocks, re-used in the inner foundations, which he sensibly identifies as a sign of Persian destruction.[84] In other words, it now seems likely that the Old Bouleuterion postdates the Persian sack of 480 and that its builders used masonry belonging to an earlier structure which the Persians had set on fire. Thompson associates this new building with the landmark reforms of Ephialtes which gave the Athenian Council sweeping new powers. We may therefore date the Council Chamber and Tholos *c.* 460 or soon thereafter. But what of the building north of the Old Bouleuterion? Since Thompson's own excavations show that it was built just after the Old Bouleuterion, it can no longer be dated *c.* 500, nor should it be absent from a plan of the Athenian Agora in the late fifth century. The excavators simply assumed, because they defined the building constructed distyle in antis as a temple, that the Persians must have destroyed it, though the building itself has yielded no trace of violent destruction, Persian or otherwise. There is accordingly no reason not to date the building to the same period as that of the Council Chamber and every archaeological obligation to do so. Moreover, no direct evidence exists which identifies this structure as a 'Temple of the Mother'. When the New Bouleuterion was built much later in the fifth century – or indeed in the fourth – the Old Bouleuterion came to be used as a public records office and at least by the mid-fourth century was known as 'the Metroon', and for two reasons: by that time it housed a statue to the Mother of the Gods introduced to Athens probably in the late fifth century and the new title could distinguish the building from the new Council Chamber to the west. When, towards the end of the second century BC, a huge new building was erected, the shrine of the Mother was located in the inner of the southern section, perhaps roughly in the same position she had previously enjoyed. The square room in the northern part of this Hellenistic building was the main record office of contemporary Athenian government and it was built over the foundations of the fifth-century building we have been discussing.[85] I therefore suggest that, like the Tholos, this other structure was not just topographically adjacent, but also functionally adjunct to the Old Bouleuterion.[86]

In a recent study of ancient archives we are told that 'the original Metroon had nothing to do with the preservation of archives'.[87] On the contrary, the building was probably erected, in an architectural style comparable with that of a state treasury, precisely in order to house the archives of the Council, the Assembly, and Athens' burgeoning Empire, and had nothing to do with the Mother of the Gods. The building was probably supervised by the official known as the 'scribe of the council' (*grammateus tes boules*) and was itself called *to demosion*, 'the public archive'. Alan Boegehold has asked why orators in the late fifth century say 'in the demosion' instead of 'in the Metroon'.[88] The answer seems simple enough: the state archive was called the *demosion*, not the Metroon, and indeed as yet had no reason to be so designated.

Ephialtes' reforms marked a turning-point in the development of Athenian constitutional government and, as a material corollary, in the history of her public building. 'The enhanced role of the Demos brought about by the democratic reforms of Ephialtes' may well, as Thompson suggests,[89] have been reflected in the programme for the construction of the new administrative centre we have described. The Tholos, built to house the council presidents, stood appropriately in front of the entrance to the Council Chamber; at its rear, an administrative annexe housed the records of the newly empowered democratic council, and other administrative structures in or near the Agora can be associated with the same building programme of civic offices (Fig. 6).[90]

Who guided this ambitious project? With Ephialtes dead and Cimon ostracized, Pericles becomes the most likely candidate to have carried forward in word and deed the reforms attributed to Ephialtes. According to Victor Ehrenberg, 'if Athens owed her empire above all to the imperialists of the fifties', the leader of the 'vigorous and resilient generation can hardly have been anyone else but Pericles'.[91] Even if Pericles in the early 450s, as Russell Meiggs has claimed, 'was not yet a dominant figure', it is likely that he had already held a generalship and, as Meiggs acknowledges, 'he had served his political apprenticeship in the sixties and had identified himself with the reforms of Ephialtes'.[92] As Myronides, Leocrates and Tolmides swayed the assembly on the basis of their military experience, Pericles may have taken his opportunity to oversee the construction of new public accommodations to meet the needs of the constitutional reforms in the achievement of which he had so closely participated. Ephialtes had 'brought the laws of Solon down to the Agora for all to see'.[93] Once Pericles had provided an efficient new civic centre for the administration of these laws, he himself returned to the Acropolis in the next decade, 'and then the works arose', as Plutarch reports, 'no less towering in their grandeur than inimitable in the grace of their outlines',[94] buildings replete with images of Greek triumph over the barbarian and the supremacy of Athenian peace.

No, Atossa, though Athens and Eretria both may have been savagely wasted by your husband and your son, Persian might did not destroy them, and today we have seen how their archaeological record may reveal something of their resilience, their imagination and political inventiveness which continue to reward the attention we are willing to pay them.

2

IMAGES OF GLORY AND THE
ART OF POWER

'Can it be that Athens' city still is undestroyed?' In the last chapter
I discussed some sacred and secular buildings in Athens or 'clearly
inspired by Athens' which, contrary to general opinion, may not
even have been built when Xerxes' 'Persepolitan' army attempted
to destroy the city. I wish to make it clear that my concern with
the dates of these buildings in no way constitutes an end in itself.
Chronological considerations are entirely subsidiary to the goal of
my study, namely, to use archaeological evidence in conjunction
with documentary sources the better to understand Athens'
cultural history, its politics, society and the aspirations of its
citizens in the first half of the fifth century. 'Men make a city, not
walls', so Thucydides asserts, and the fabric of political institutions
or state and private cults does not necessarily depend upon their
material accommodation. Nonetheless, buildings and other kinds
of monument reflect needs and priorities significant at the time of
their erection, and in order to recover something of those concerns
we must first commit ourselves to reconstructing, within the limits
of the available evidence, their likely chronological setting.

On a related issue, P.J. Rhodes rightly observes that 'we ought
not to persist in ascribing the prytany system, with its rotating
committee of council presidents, to Cleisthenes, merely because it
accords with our idea of what he was trying to do.' Rhodes argues
that this particular organizational model may in fact not have been
introduced until Ephialtes' reforms of 462 and so suggests that
year as a *terminus post quem* for the building of the Tholos as
meeting-place for these presidents of council.[1] In a recent
collection of essays entitled *Athens Comes of Age*, T. Leslie Shear, Jr
– on no direct evidence, for, as Rhodes had stressed, none exists –
nonetheless prefers the traditional view that the prytany system

21

had been established nearly half a century earlier by the legislation of Cleisthenes. For the Tholos, he therefore maintains the historically unmotivated date of 'around 465' first proposed by Homer Thompson, its excavator.[2] Leslie Shear, the current director of the Agora excavations, also maintains the standard, Cleisthenic date for the Old Bouleuterion at 'the end of the sixth century',[3] again first proposed by Homer Thompson, his predecessor at the Agora.

Homer Thompson, as we have seen, now associates the Old Bouleuterion and the Tholos (Fig. 6) with Ephialtes' reform of the Council's constitutional power, citing the re-use of fire-damaged masonry in the Council Chamber's inner foundations.[4] We have seen too that the structure immediately to the north of the Old Bouleuterion, built soon afterwards, but as a part of the same construction programme, was probably Athens' public record office. I suggested at the end of the last chapter that rather than wait until the closing decade of the fifth century for a centralized archive, the Athenians constructed a building for this very purpose around 460, at the beginning of the decade in which Athens also seems to have centralized the administration of her Empire.[5] The probability that, in the period before the Persian Wars, laws and other documentary archives may have been kept in the archaic Temple of Athena on the Acropolis destroyed by the Persians by no means requires us to suppose that when, in Anaximenes' words, 'Ephialtes transferred the state archives from up on the Acropolis to the Bouleuterion and the Agora',[6] he installed them in another sanctuary, rather than in the building next to the Bouleuterion and which the Athenians themselves probably knew as their *demosion*. I shall therefore not again use 'Metroon' as a term for this structure, not least because we have no evidence that it was ever so called in ancient Athens or was in any way associated with the Mother of the Gods.

Now, whether or not Pericles was the prime mover in these events, we gain a revised picture of civic leadership at Athens in the early 450s, not to mention the administration of her democratic institutions, if a new civic centre (including judiciary offices, council chamber with its presidential hall and a public records office attached to it, and the provision of a formal meeting place for the Athenian Assembly on the Pnyx)[7] was constructed in response to constitutional reforms achieved in the years immediately preceding the production of Aeschylus' *Oresteia* and constituted part of an integrated, political programme for the government not only of a city, but of its new Empire. And before we leave this cluster of civic buildings in the southwest corner of the Agora, let us remember that they belong to the second period of the public works programme in which the construction of the Great Drain was the first priority. To quote the *Agora Guide*, 'the exact correspondence in orientation between the Drain and the Old Bouleuterion . . . as well as the stratification between the two, shows that they are parts of one and the same program conceived with a view to a more commodious and monumental Agora'.[8] Thompson's point is well taken since, during heavy rains, before the Drain was built, the area of the Agora was liable to become an incommodious swamp, a condition which the Drain was designed to correct, by collecting 'the waters which still today pour down in great torrents after rainstorm from the Areopagus and nearby hills'.[9] We might compare a similar structure under the barracks at Persepolis[10] and speculate that the line of the Drain was dug some twenty years before by Xerxes' army during the Persian occupation of Athens. This and other possible activities connected with the Athenian water-supply on the part of the skilled hydraulic engineers whom Xerxes had included in his invasion force have been discussed elsewhere.[11] The great square shaft at Sunium may also have been constructed by Persian engineers on the edge of the Laurian silver mines to release that *argyrou pege*, 'a mine of treasure in the earth, a fount of silver ore'.[12]

But back to Athens and the point of these introductory remarks. In reflecting at a distance of fifty years upon his initial reconstruction of the history of the democratic buildings I have been discussing, Homer Thompson recalls, for example, in the case of the Ekklesia on the Pnyx that 'the excavators were . . . driven to rely largely on *historical probability* [my italics] in proposing even a tentative date for Period I' and they took the democratic reforms of Cleisthenes to provide 'the most probable occasion'.[13] Now that archaeological evidence has persuaded Professor Thompson to revise his initial impressions, it seems to me that a far more convincing 'historical probability' has been attained. Instead of assuming that Athens' civic centre sprang fully furbished from the head of Cleisthenes, we can now attribute it to the period when Athenian democracy, if not Athens herself, 'came of age' in the political reorganization which indeed consolidated her people in their new power.

Lest these considerations appear to have little to do with 'Images of glory and the art of power', let me repeat the point which justifies their discussion: unless one is going to study Greek art in a timeless and purely stylometric context, concentrating on technical execution and its measurement, then it becomes essential to try to identify the historical circumstances which may have contributed, for example, to the erection of public buildings and which their decoration may reflect. The probable misidentification of Athens' *demosion* in terms of both time and function has, at the very least, led students of Greek religion to suppose that the Athens of Cleisthenes instituted the worship of an otherwise alien goddess in the midst of her civic centre — and if this anomaly has had scant effect upon our understanding of Athenian social history, it is only because, with notable exceptions, Greek religion has not usually been studied from this perspective.

And so to some images of glory and the art of power in a society in which, public archives or no, literacy was by no means yet widespread and the spoken word and visual image still remained complementary and basic vehicles of public information. At the end of his recent history of modern art, *The Shock of the New*, Richard Hughes has well defined this capacity of word and image not only to inform taste, but also under conditions that prevailed, for example, in fifteenth-century Italy and seventeenth-century Flanders, to command mass social and religious conviction. Works of art, like Carpaccio's *Legend of St Ursula* 'whose message to us has no more reality than a fairy tale' could, so Hughes observes, 'acquire for the audience of their time the force of history and the augury of revelation. [Public art] made legends tangible and credible, inserting them unconditionally into the lives of their audience, compelling belief and [directing] behavior. That', writes Hughes in his epilogue on 'The Future that was', 'was what public art has always been meant to do',[14] and that, I believe, is what it did in fifth-century Athens.

I recognize that the interpretation of iconography (as of literature) can involve an element of subjectivity, but I take encouragement from Jasper Griffin's recommendation of Colin Macleod's passing remark about the reading of poetry: 'it is less unfaithful to the object', Macleod observes with simple truth, 'to make subjective comments than to abstain from comment altogether'.[15] In discussing the Temple of Apollo at Eretria (pp. 8–15), I assumed that its decoration was originally expressed according to a unified compositional programme designed to reinforce a manifesto reflecting the interests of those who had authorised the temple's construction. I found it hardly surprising that the Eretrian gable we looked at in the last chapter offers (to my eyes, at least) a richer commentary on the nature of the Athenian alliance following the sack of Sardis and the battle of Marathon, where the archaeological evidence may place it, than is allowed by its traditional date in the years preceding the Ionian Revolt in the years before Athens and Eretria had first joined forces against an eastern foe. Whatever may have been the decoration of the eastern gable, the western, facing towards Attica, asserts the might of Athens' warrior goddess, Polias 'defender of cities', and the enterprise of Theseus, her national hero. If some form of iconographic self-reference to Eretria was included in the scene (for example, the loss of her field-general in the battle of Ephesus),[16] it has not been preserved. What little remains of the whole suggests an open acknowledgement of Athenian initiative, but mention of Eualcidas prompts me to dwell briefly on the particular appropriateness of the image as a monument to the Ionian escapade I referred to in the last chapter.

The Athenian fleet with its Eretrian escort of five warships crossed the Aegean for their landfall at Ephesus where the troops disembarked. Ephesian guides conducted the troops up-country, cresting the ridge of Mt Tmolus above the Persian satrapy capital of Sardis. They set the city on fire, but were unable to capture the Persian garrison and, as reinforcements arrived, the Greeks retreated back across Tmolus and rejoined their ships. The Persians pursued the commandos to Ephesus and trounced them in the ensuing battle among whose dead Herodotus remembers Eualcidas, the Eretrian commander, a renowned athletic victor, celebrated by Simonides.[17] At this reverse the Greek fleet sailed for home, abandoning the Ionian cause. In Greek tradition, so Devambez and others have demonstrated,[18] Ephesus had strong Amazonian associations, 'and we might remember', with John Boardman, 'that when the Athenians burned the temple of Cybele-Artemis at Sardis, they destroyed a temple of the goddess of the Amazons'.[19] If any Greek casualties were represented on the west gable at Eretria, victims of the Amazon archer (Fig. 3), then a contemporary onlooker might well remember Ephesus and, in particular, Eretrian Eualcidas. The involvement of Athens and Eretria in this Ionian episode is recounted by Herodotus in less than flattering terms,[20] but 'in Athens', Boardman well observes, 'the whole affair, an exceptionally bold one in terms of resources and distances, must have been regarded as a sharp lesson to arrogant barbarians by the new democracy in support of her kin overseas'.[21]

It will by now be clear that, to the extent an image may reflect upon the cultural history of a community, its ideological significance depends on basic considerations of time, of place, and of its iconographic setting. The fact that Athena commands the Eretrian gable does not of itself entitle us to conclude that its pedimental decoration was 'inspired by Athens'; it is her collocation with the Attic hero, Theseus, which suggests that an enterprise in which Athens played a distinctive role has been thus memorialized. At Aegina, for example, both pediments are dominated by Athena's presence, but now apparently in the company of her native sons, Ajax and his father, Telamon. What is Athena's role at Aegina? This is not the occasion to rehearse all the difficulties involved in any attempt to reconstruct the history of the temple decorated by the famous Aeginetan Marbles (Fig. 7). As Ephorus remarked, 'in the case of events long ago we hold that those who go into details are the least to be believed',[22] but it is now generally thought that the building dates from the end of the sixth century and that its pedimental decoration was completed by the 470s.[23]

Throughout this period, Aegina's international policy favoured Sparta and Thebes, while relations between Athens and her powerful island neighbour across the bay were marked by enmity and open warfare. At the end of the century, Aeginetan marauders harassed the Attic coastline, in 490 she 'gave earth and water' to Persia, and Athens even persuaded the Spartan king, Cleomenes, to demand hostages as a guarantee of her neutrality. Once the hostages were returned, Aegina reopened hostilities as Athens unsuccessfully interfered in her internal politics by supporting Nicodromus' attempt to lead the democratic faction into power. Themistocles appealed to the Athenians to use their silver strike at Laurium to build a fleet against this constant Aeginetan threat and so on the eve of the second Persian invasion enforced peace between the two states. In 480 it was Thebes, not Aegina, who consorted with the enemy. Aegina for her part sent a squadron to the Greek fleet at Salamis and she won the greatest distinction for her valour in the naval action. Next year she shared in the victory at Plataea and her fleet participated in early league activities in Cyprus and the Euxine in 478, wintering at the Thessalian port of Pagasae in the following year. Nonetheless, Russell Meiggs argues from Thucydides' testimony that 'Aegina, with the other Peloponnesians, left the Greek fleet before the oaths of allegiance were exchanged'.[24] Her continuing hostility towards Athens is evidenced by her support of Sparta in opposing Themistocles' decision to fortify Athens and, in Meiggs' view, she appears unlikely to have joined the Athenian Confederacy until coerced to do so in the 450s. On the other hand, despite Meiggs' understandable exasperation with Diodorus' muddled account on which the matter rests,[25] Douglas MacDowell makes a strong case for concluding 'that Aegina was one of the original members of the Delian League'.[26]

Can these considerations affect our understanding of the Aeginetan Marbles? The temple, as I have mentioned, is conventionally dated later than Apollo's temple at Eretria. The west pediment with Ajax is thought on stylistic grounds to belong to the 490s and the east pediment, with Ajax's father, Telamon, to the following decade and there is some question that it may have replaced an earlier programme.[27] These were not years in which Aegina is likely to have intended Athena as a tribute to Athens, and her martial presence is therefore usually interpreted as a reference to her unremitting efforts on behalf of the Greek cause at Troy. In these terms one might even think of her image as a gesture not of détente, but of defiance towards Athens who had by contrast so small a part to play at Troy. The previous temple on this site appears to have been dedicated not to Athena, but to Aphaia, a local nymph about whose cult and character we are, to say the least, ill-informed. Aphaia continued to receive dedicatory offerings in the fifth century and we do not know what position, if any, Athena commanded in the liturgy of this new temple, but if Athena usurped her role, she did so only partially.

Why was this new temple built? Dyfri Williams has suggested that c. 510 the previous one may have been struck by lightning,[28] but I know of no evidence, archaeological or meteorological, which requires this chronological hypothesis. Indeed, in default of clear evidence to the contrary, might it not be that the possibility of a post-Marathonian date for the sculpture of Apollo's temple at Eretria encourages a return to the suggestion canvassed in the nineteenth century[29] that the temple was erected to commemorate

Aegina's distinguished contribution to Greek victory at Salamis on which island Ajax, albeit of Aeginetan lineage, had formerly dwelt?[30] Indeed Herodotus reports[31] that the most notable 'first fruits' of the plunder taken in battle and offered to the gods as tokens of thanksgiving were three Phoenician warships, one of which was dedicated on Salamis itself in honour of Ajax, her most celebrated hero.

Aegina took understandable pride in her success, as she evidently did in the memory that Telamon had accompanied Heracles in the first expedition, and that Telamon's son, Ajax, and his nephew, Achilles, had been so instrumental in achieving victory for the Atreids in the next generation. 'In choosing his myths for Aegina', Bowra once wrote, 'Pindar is moved by the desire to show that the glorious past is alive in the present, and descent from heroes makes the Aeginetans what they are.'[32] When Pindar contemplated 'a victor, he evidently conceived him as from a certain city, reared in its cults and inspired by its heroes; his victory would in some sense be simultaneously theirs.'[33] In his fourth *Nemean Ode*, Pindar accordingly sends Ajax and Telamon in turn to Cyprus, to Salamis, the Euxine, and to Thessaly, and in the fifth *Isthmian*, composed for another Aeginetan victor, possibly in 478, this is how he mediates his return to the present, epinician occasion from a myth celebrating Telamon and Ajax who 'after much fighting twice sacked the Trojans' town': '*kai nun*, and even now, Salamis, city of Ajax, could bear witness that she was saved from shipwreck in war by Aegina's seamen in that destroying storm of Zeus which death came thick as hail on hosts unnumbered.'[34] Salaminian Ajax was undoubtedly a hero in whom Aegina had long felt pride, but is it not possible that just as the fourth *Nemean* casts the recent success of Aegina's navy in terms of mythical Aeacid enterprise, so the Aeginetan pediments celebrate Aegina's role in Greece's triumph over an Asiatic foe?

Herodotus may indirectly provide a clue which helps us understand how the Aeginetans built their temple:

> After the first-fruits [*scil.*, from the victory at Salamis] had been sent to Delphi, the Greeks made inquiry of the god, in the name of their whole body, if he had received his full share of the spoils and was satisfied therewith. The god made answer, that all the other Greeks had paid him his full due,

except only the Aeginetans; on them he still had a claim for
the prize of valour which they had gained at Salamis. So the
Aeginetans, when they heard this, dedicated the three golden
stars which stand on the top of a bronze mast.[35]

One may wonder whether Aeacid Neoptolemus' 'wrangling with
the temple ministers [of Delphi] concerning due apportionment of
honour' – in a *Paean* for the Delphians arguably composed in
thanksgiving for deliverance from the Persian menace – might be
Pindar's way of alluding to Aegina's debt.[36] At any rate, the
Aeginetan offering, however symbolically appropriate,[37] cannot
have seemed an especially lavish one for a god to whom, as for
Odysseus, it was the value of the gift and not the thought that
counted. It may well be 'probable', as Blakesley suggested in
1854, 'that their gratitude was more ready on their own soil', and
that they spent their winnings on refurbishing their temple and
decorating it with heroic images reflective of their glory.[38]
Pointing out that Aegina's economy traditionally depended on
trade with the east, Meiggs suggests plausible reasons why 'Aegina
could have had a very practical interest in carrying the war against
Persia into the eastern Mediterranean'.[39] If Aegina was indeed, as
Diodorus implies and MacDowell has argued, an early member of
the Delian League, then Athena's leadership would be no less
appropriate to current political realities than to mythical
precedent. In both endeavours, Athena relied upon Aeginetan
heroes and directs them in successful exploits against a common,
oriental foe.

No one has ever doubted that all but one of the monuments I
shall discuss in the next three chapters postdate the Persian Wars.
With the Temple at Aegina, certainty seems at present
unattainable,[40] but the hypothesis I have suggested accounts for
what evidence we have. No doubt, some will prefer to interpret
the relationship between the Aeginetan pediments and Pindaric
inspiration as Jebb did when he suggested 'that the poet's
immediate theme may have occurred to his mind as he gazed on
the sculptor's work in the splendid entablature of the temple'.[41]
The chronological relationship I am proposing, however, has a
close parallel in the relationship between the subject matter of
Pindar's tenth Olympian (celebrating a victory won in 476) and
the subsequent construction of the temple of Zeus at Olympia. At

least I do not readily see how the stylistic 'contrast between the two [Aeginetan pediments]', described as a contrast between 'the Archaic and the imminent Classical'[42] necessarily requires us to date them apart. No one seriously doubts that the friezes of the Siphnian Treasury which also exhibit differing styles belong to the same building programme and the same may well be true at Aegina. In any case, at Aegina it is the stylistically 'archaic' pediment which I have suggested as an image of Salamis.

My hesitation to insist on these conclusions reminds me of a reported exchange between Cecil Rhodes and Lord Acton: 'Why doesn't Theodore Bent say straight out that those ruins of his in Mashonaland are Phoenician?' Cecil Rhodes inquired. 'I suppose', Lord Acton replied, 'that he is not quite sure that they are Phoenician.' 'Ah!' said Rhodes, 'that's not the way Empires are built.' How true. Empires are built by the method Wilamowitz so admired in Adolf Furtwängler, the archaeologist whom he singles out for special mention in his *Geschichte der Philologie* as 'the one scholar who had a truly synoptic view of the whole and who tried to reduce it to order by main force [*gewaltsam*] (the only way)'.[43] We saw in Chapter 1 what 'main force' could effect at Eretria, and even today, when the Aeginetan evidence remains far from definitive, I would still prefer to seek order in a world where victors use their spoils to enhance their local sanctuaries than one in which the archaeologist feels entitled to invoke as *deus ex machina* Zeus' lightning bolts to destroy an old temple (from which no evidence of violent destruction exists) simply because our stylistic chronology has ordered up a new one.

'Can it be that Athens' city still is undestroyed?' How could Atossa appear so ill-informed? For, as Herodotus recalls, 'Xerxes' . . . dispatch telling of the capture of Athens caused such rejoicing in Susa amongst the Persians who had not accompanied the expedition, that they strewed the roads with myrtle-boughs, burned incense, and gave themselves up to every sort of pleasure and merrymaking.'[44] But our Atossa was not in Susa, she was upon the tragic stage in Athens, and I must now discuss two important questions I mentioned in the last chapter which some may think I have already ignored to the detriment of this argument: first, the possibility, not the necessity, that a relationship may exist between poetry and contemporary events, and, second, the reconciliation, in Jasper Griffin's words, of 'heroic myths with the world of ordinary experience and history'.[45]

In defence of his recent protest against what he styles *The Enemies of Poetry*, W.B. Stanford declared that

> antipoetic forces are still so strongly entrenched in classical
> studies that to make any lasting impression on them one
> must thrust hard [to prevent the advocates of history and
> politics among others from trying] to convert and assimilate
> poetry to their own purposes. . . . All I assert is the
> uniqueness and autonomy of poetry'[46]

or, as he puts it elsewhere, 'hands off, historians'. Knowing that the Grantchester clock actually registered 'half past three', some of you may have wondered how I can include reference to Aeschylus and Pindar in an essentially historical study. In many of you, Stanford's jeremiad will have struck a responsive chord (rather than caught a nerve) for scholars nowadays will often seek to protect Athenian tragedy in particular from those who would read it as a form of political allegory and, as latter-day Telchines, mine its texts as quarries of historical information about contemporary events.

In his article entitled 'Politics and the *Oresteia*', Colin Macleod has once again surely stated the issue with correctness and tact:

> the tragedian is influenced by his time and circumstances;
> but they are an influence on the work, not the meaning of it.
> And it is only through an examination of that meaning that
> both the lasting greatness of the poet and his position in his
> own time and city can be illuminated.[47]

But this is not to say that some of the political circumstances of the poet's own time and culture are not reflected through the influences of which Macleod writes. And similar considerations may apply to epinician and dithyrambic verse; however much 'the lasting greatness' of such poetry transcends the occasion it was created to celebrate. Macleod's teacher, Eduard Fraenkel, addressed himself to this question of influence more directly in evaluating the significance of Karl Otfried Müller's edition of Aeschylus' *Eumenides* which gave rise to such storms of protest when it appeared in 1833:

> Henceforth, no conscientious scholar was at liberty to
> comment on a Greek play without taking into account the
> monuments of art as well as the literature, or to neglect the

relevant problems of religion, law, and political and social history, and the conditions of performances on the Athenian stage.[48]

'Tragedy may well', as Günther Zuntz observes, 'absorb the living forces of its day into the absolute sphere of the myth'.[49] Those 'living forces', however, so much a part of the current memory of the playwright's audience, provide much of the energy that made the Greek theatre so effective an instrument of reflection, as when, for example, Euripides' Cassandra, speaking from a beleaguered city, on the eve of the Sicilian expedition, eloquently argues her plea for a military policy of self-defence in preference to a war of aggression (*Trojan Women* 400). While it would be foolish to suppose that Aeschylus' Atossa upon her tragic stage in any way contradicts an historian's testimony concerning Susa's knowledge of the sack of Athens, the Persian Wars did nonetheless provide the historical context from which Aeschylus' *Persians* unfolds.

Xerxes' atrocities against the shrines and olive groves of Attica are duly told by the Ghost of Darius rising from his tomb, and when we, as Athenians, hear Darius' warning, 'be mindful of the men of Greece and Athens, lest one among you, disdaining in his mind the fortune of the present and lusting after more, waste the great blessings he has',[50] we should also take heed lest we too behave like Persians who, by nature, are prone to acts of *hybris* that brings as its crop, the full harvest of *ate*.[51] We know well enough that the excess of Xerxes' sacrilege at the sack of Athens brought about his inevitable catastrophe. So too, if a Greek behaves like a Persian, he can expect that Zeus *dikaios* will not spare him merely on account of his Hellenic blood, and part of Aeschylus' point in *Agamemnon* is that the king does indeed behave as orientals would or as they have done.

We are not surprised when we find the influence of Homer's *Iliad* evident in Aeschylean drama. So when Clytemnestra begins her speech at line 281 by invoking Hephaestus, 'sending forth from Ida a bright radiance' which *ap' angarou puros* is transmitted first to 'Hermes' rock on Lemnos' (line 283) and thence to 'Zeus' peak of Athos' (line 285) we remember the passage in the second book of the *Iliad*[52] in which the same trinity had authorized the house of Pelops to rule at Argos. In the *Iliad* Hephaestus had wrought the sceptre which Agamemnon by rightful inheritance now wields. The repetition of *eskepsen* (lines 302 and 308) and *skeptei* (line 310) to which Fraenkel draws attention[53] invites comparison between Hephaestus' two gifts, the Iliadic *skeptron* and the Aeschylean *skeptos*, both of them reflecting the prerogative of Agamemnon's power which Clytemnestra plots to usurp. Let us, however, also heed Fraenkel's counsel to consider how social and religious history may influence our understanding of a Greek play. The Athenian interest in fostering the cult of Pan after his epiphany to the original 'Marathon man' is evident in poetry and art.[54] So when the war was over, in recompense for past neglect and thanksgiving for services the god had rendered, the Athenians 'made a sanctuary for Pan in a cave under the Acropolis and appeased him with annual sacrifices and a torch-race'.[55] Did this contemporary attention to the mountain god, newly significant in the doxology of Marathon, possibly influence Aeschylus when in the opening chorus of the *Agamemnon* we find him, set beside Zeus and Apollo, as a 'being on high' who hears the cries of suppliants?[56]

Herodotus, however, has a torch-race to another god in mind, one held in honour of Hephaestus and to which Clytemnestra also may allude,[57] when he described the Persian system of communication which did not rely on the spirit of a lone man running for his country's life, but operated through relays of horsemen. In Persia, this courier service, the fastest mode of travel in Herodotus' world, which the Achaemenids seem to have adopted from Babylonian antecedents,[58] was called by a term Greeks rendered as *angareion*.[59] And Xerxes used the system to announce first his capture of Athens and then his defeat at Salamis. Mardonius, left in command, 'set his heart', so Herodotus reports, 'upon taking Athens again, . . . in part because he desired to signal his capture of the town to the king in Sardis by a chain of beacons *(pursoisi dia neson)'*.[60] And since the Greek fleet now controlled the islands of the Aegean at least west of Delos, this chain would probably have followed much the same line as that of Agamemnon's beacons, which communicated to his own queen in Argos the news that Troy had fallen.[61] We are accustomed to think of beacon lights in the *Agamemnon* as a signal of salvation out of the darkness of chaos, the bright blaze of Hephaestus, but to an Athenian for whom Xerxes' abominable destruction was scarcely twenty years old, Agamemnon's choice of telegraphy must have had a more ominous tone than it can have for us. Not only the technique, but the word Clytemnestra uses is borrowed from Iran;

angarou in the phrase *ap' angarou puros* at line 282 in *Agamemnon* is a patent loan-word in Greek which invokes, at its Old Persian source, exactly the Achaemenian courier system I have just mentioned while linking the *angareion* with the system of beaconing (cf. *puros*) which the author *de Mundo* ascribes to the Achaemenid kings from Cambyses to Xerxes.[62] While the Greeks themselves are said to have used flares at this period (for example, Diodorus attributes such action to Cimon at the Eurymedon)[63] Hellenic telegraphy differs both in scale and function. So when Miltiades spotted a forest fire on Mykonos across the water from Paros, he reportedly believed he had intercepted a beacon signalling Persian intervention.[64]

In her speech at line 320, Clytemnestra cynically imagines her husband's acts of sacrilege against Troy. It is no accident that Agamemnon's messenger joyously authenticates her predictions and that both speeches draw much of their diction from the language of Xerxes' sack of Athens in Aeschylus' *Persians*. When Agamemnon himself returns, his concubine Cassandra alights from a carriage described in line 1054 as an *hamaxeres thronos*. The word *thronos* is self-evidently ominous, and Alföldi has convincingly suggested that the conveyance refers to the throne wagon, the *harmamaxa*, which Xerxes used on campaigns,[65] but which in Herodotus and Aristophanes (for example, in the *Acharnians*) is more often a carriage of the Achaemenian king's mistress, and in such a carriage Themistocles was conveyed to Susa. Agamemnon is thus characterized as an oriental potentate from the moment he comes on stage, and ironically it is from such a vehicle that he first recoils in disgust at being subjected to the *proskynesis* of his subjects and to the carpeted path that welcomed his return. The Argive chorus at lines 367–402 had already characterized the Trojans in terms of the arrogant and luxurious decadence which, to a Greek audience of the early 450s, typified oriental society. Agamemnon, in conquering the Trojans, had from an ethical standpoint become one of them. 'What would Priam have done?' asks Clytemnestra (lines 935–6). 'I think for sure', replies Agamemnon, 'that he would have walked upon the embroideries', and Agamemnon promptly does likewise, vainly, but consciously praying that 'no glance of envious eye strike me from afar' (lines 946–7).[66] You will say that Priam is a Trojan, not a Persian, but, apart from the evidence of visual art, I can only refer you, if not to Aegina, to Helen Bacon's clear demonstration, from the study of Aeschylean

and Sophoclean fragments, that the world of Troy is characteristically expressed by reference to the world of contemporary Persia.
'Sophocles' Trojans', Bacon tells us, 'speak a Persian language,
refer to Persian objects, and observe Persian customs, or what
passed for Persian among fifth-century Greeks instructed by
Aeschylus, Hecataeus, and Herodotus.'[67]

'Did the Greeks believe their own myths?' the *Times Literary
Supplement* recently invited us to inquire.[68] While the word 'belief'
in such a context may have distracting overtones, myths were
indeed, to quote Jasper Griffin's review, 'a special form of story'.[69]
Would Xenophanes and Pindar have inveighed with such
insistence against these 'deceptive fictions' if they merely
entertained and did not more profoundly mould the moral
attitudes of many Greeks?[70] At the beginning of the fifth century,
myth was probably still for most Greeks an extraordinarily potent
means of expressing and informing their experience of the
world.[71] Most of the rest of what I have to say in this book will
presuppose a special relationship between myth and history
whereby particular myths were selected and at times recast so that
they might be perceived as prefigurations of recent and present
events.

We have heard Pindar use this style of discourse in praising the
athletes of Aegina, but while the Apolline poet may conceive that
his god's capacity as an archer *hekatebeletes* to shoot straight though
from afar upon his target equally expresses the activity of his
intelligence, we shall defeat ourselves if we always demand of myth
what John Finley calls 'the precision of reference, the capacity to
signify one thing and one thing only . . . which philosophers and
logicians have come to admire as the sole reliable ground of
reference.'[72] Traditional myths – as opposed to those invented in
order to promote the cult-propaganda of a god or of a man – will
often not allow one to isolate a specific reconciliation between their
own terms of reference and those of actuality. It was in fact the
attempt to explore the possibility of deriving such precise relations
between categories that led Greeks, and at first the sophists, to
abandon traditional patterns of mythological discourse in favour of
a new, more specific style of definition by category, and, perhaps
significantly, the allegorical interpretation of myth played an early
and important part in this process. Nonetheless, the mythical
mode of expression possessed in power and suggestiveness what it
may have lacked in precision. No matter that in detail the Persian

Wars from Marathon to Plataea are, for the most part, not strictly comparable with traditions of the Greek siege and sack of Troy; the analogy of a decade of war between Hellene and barbarian from which Greece each time emerged victorious after much privation and acts of individual heroism, this analogy was sufficient to give the comparison force.

I therefore intend to examine this use of mythological imagery as a reflection of the historical event of the recent military triumphs over Persia, for by such means, in a culture largely instructed by visual images and the formally spoken word, the Greeks not only gloried in their victory, but derived a paradigm of the conduct to be excluded from their gates, if their society was to survive the hazard of invasion from without or within. And so, Agamemnon, disregarding his own knowledge, the conqueror conquered, steps upon the royal tapestries and on to his fateful bath where Clytemnestra 'spread the endless casting-net around him, as men do for fishes',[73] and herself – not Aegisthus, as on the Dokimasia Painter's Boston crater – stabs him thrice.[74]

'Philology without a view of art', Goethe once proclaimed, 'is but one-eyed'.[75] Hitherto, I have argued conversely that 'Kunstbegriff ohne Philologie ist einäugig', but lest I be mistaken for a Cyclopean goat or, worse still, a latter-day King's Eyed Pseudartabas who gives false measure, I shall close this discourse on *Philologie* with a coda of *Kunstbegriff*. First, if I may, I shall emulate the athletic inspiration of Pindar's Aeacid eagle who, in another Aeginetan ode, sang:

Dig me a pit for leaping. The spring in my knees is light[76]

and climb aboard that estimable bird to leave behind the fifth century for a few minutes and take you to the second half of the fourth, for the Darius Painter was active in Southern Italy during the lifetime of Alexander. He is known for his enormous volute craters; one of them depicts the Trojan War and the funeral pyre of Patroclus, another, by which he is known, the Court of Darius at the moment of decision before the king's army marched forth to Marathon (Fig. 8).[77]

On the body of this vase the painter has arranged his scenes in three levels, an image of social order in which the world of men is subject to divine authority. The drama is simultaneous rather than expressive of a narrative sequence. In the highest register we see the gods; at the bottom, humanity congregates at the secular shrine of the imperial treasury and, in the centre, Darius, so named and mighty among men, sits upon a golden throne, his royal sceptre in his right hand. In the starry heaven of the divine zone and directly above the Persian monarch, Zeus sits enthroned likewise holding his sceptre. The thunderbolt with which he will smite Persia rests between his throne and the figure of Greece to his left. On his right winged Victory leans against his knee, ready to fly. Zeus extends his free hand towards Greece who thus stands secure between the Father of Gods and Men and his daughter Athena in full battle-dress. Athena's right hand rests protectively on Greece's shoulder. Guarded by gods on either hand Greece carries no sceptre for, by contrast with Darius' Persia, she is a community of the free. The divine siblings, Apollo and Artemis, mistress of animals, sit to the right of their father because it was on the day of Artemis that the Battle of Marathon was fought. Asia sits outside the Olympian group to their left, facing, however, in their direction. She is seated before the herm-shaped altar of Aphrodite, national goddess of Asia, and, in front of her, disguised as a Fury with snakes in her hair, the personification of Delusion (*Apate*) incites her to ruin by casting the torch of war between the incipient combatants. As Delusion moves in the direction of the central group her head is turned back towards Asia whose eyes and those of Aphrodite are fixed upon her face. 'All unrestrained lust and hope of wealth and glory', writes Porphyry, 'derive from [evil daemons], and chief among these is Delusion.'[78] The continents, Greece and Asia, define the scene of conflict, Delusion, its ethical cause. Significantly enough, Athena stands between Asia and Greece with her head turned towards the continent she will protect.

In the central zone Darius is enthroned amidst his counsellors. He is facing a figure standing on a circular platform, whom Hinks has interpreted as the collective expression of the Persian people.[79] He is an old man and wears travelling boots. His journey is indeed a perilous one for the raised fingers of his right hand may be intended to suggest not the traditional sign of greeting, but a gesture of admonition. H.Brunn has seen in this central group a pictorial illustration of an Achaemenid court practice later reported by Aelian:

if someone wished to counsel the Persian king on particularly

37

secret or ambiguous matters, he had to do so standing upon a golden plinth. If his counsel was considered good, he took the plinth away with him as his reward, but he was scourged nonetheless for he had spoken against the king.[80]

We therefore see Darius' guard standing behind the throne with his sword raised at the ready. Cornford aptly recalls the warning which the aged Artabanus, brother of Darius, offered Xerxes, equally to no effect.[81] In any case, if the old man's purpose is to advise the king against his mission to Greece, he has come too late for Delusion already moves towards a declaration of war, and we may recall a passage from the opening chorus of Aeschylus' *Persians* here quoted in Morshead's quaint verse:

Stern is the onset of Persia, and gallant her children in fight.
But the guile of the god is deceitful, and who shall elude him
  in flight?
And who is the lord of the leap, that can spring and alight
  and evade,
For Ate deludes and allures, till round him the meshes are laid
And no man his doom can escape.[82]

In the lowest register, we see the accumulation of wealth as the tribute money of a vassal empire comes tumbling into the imperial coffers supervised by Darius the Shopkeeper's accountant. The tribute-bearers are variously attired, their costume – as at Persepolis, but in accordance with Greek stylistic conventions – representing different regions of the empire. Within the treasury where the accountant keeps track of the tribute to the last farthing, one vassal brings a bag of money, the other, three golden cups. Outside three more orientals grovel empty-handed in traditional *proskynesis*, reminding us of the inexorable ruthlessness of the treatment which those who did not meet their tribute quotas might expect. As we have noted, in the council of gods above the world of mortals, the die is already cast and the specific day foretold, a powerful expression of fate. On the other hand, between the Olympian zone and that of ordinary humanity, Darius is still in his palace; he is not yet dressed for war. If he could only look around the vase to the scene on the reverse or up to its neck (Figs 9 and 10), he would see Bellerophon slaying the asiatic chimaera and the Greeks laying waste the Amazons. Perhaps he would not have sent his armies forth along the Royal Road to defeat and, had he not done so, Athens and the Athenian fifth century would probably not be ours today.

But march he did, and back in Athens after the war, we again see the Triptolemus Painter's image of a Greek hoplite in the moment of victory (Fig. 11),[83] delivering the *coup de grâce* to his Persian victim who, despite his outlandish costume, has been a worthy adversary, still defiant in defeat. The scene is obviously an historical, not a mythical one, yet the Greek displays upon his shield the token of Athena's support, for it was she who first enabled Bellerophon, foe of Amazons, to bridle Pegasus and so ride him east to slay the chimaera. But on a jug in Hamburg (Fig. 12)[84] we see a different image of the oriental in the aftermath of his defeat at the Eurymedon. Here again we see a victorious Greek, but girt no longer as a hoplite. The oriental's name is 'Eurymedon', his arms are raised in a gesture iconographically characteristic of women and barbarians, both of them *habroi*,[85] and his body assumes a posture in which Sir Kenneth Dover would find no self-respecting *pais kalos*.[86] Passive and unresisting he waits for a different *coup de grâce*, or to quote the title of a review in the *Times Literary Supplement*, 'a phallocratic backlash'.

On Greek vases contemporary barbarians will wear their native costumes as part of their characterization. Amazons too are attired like other archers in the Persian army, but when we move to the world of myth, different conditions seem to apply. First of all, what is the principle involved? Are we in fact entitled to suppose that the decoration of a Greek pot is more than merely decorative? And if we reconstruct a compositional programme by which various scenes on a single vessel may be interrelated, is the sum of the whole greater than that of its parts? Can we read such iconographic texts as sufficient entities in themselves? Do comparable considerations obtain when we turn from a large, public monument like a temple, to a small, privately owned object like a drinking-cup which so obviously lacks the Darius Painter's narrative scale? Yet it is not unreasonable to compare the epigrammatic form of such a vessel with that of a drinking song, and to suppose that pot-painters decorated their work with scenes variously appropriate to the vessel's use or the social and political preoccupations of their Athenian clientele.

Assigning absolute dates to Greek vase-paintings is not an easy undertaking. Of the two images of the Sack of Troy illustrated in Figs 13 and 14[87] one is conventionally dated after the sack of

Athens, the other at least ten years before. I do not consider myself to have violated any valid principle of method by proposing that the stylistically more conservative vessel may have been executed at approximately the same time as the younger one and reflects a similar, ideological response to the recent sack of Athens. And, for reasons that will become clear in the next chapter. I think it more likely that Theseus met his stepmother Amphitrite after Athens became a maritime power rather than before.

I am suggesting that, once again, considerations of time, place and iconographic context are essential to our ability to decipher these images. At the point at which we can observe some significant reorganization of conventional subjects and especially the introduction of new ones, it may be well to look beyond the artist's studio for their explanation. Theseus' victory over the Minotaur as the dénouement of his heroic enterprise had long been a popular subject in Greek vase-painting. Why, all of a sudden, did this change come about? Did the decorators merely cast around in their repertoire of myths and ring a change for the sake of change? Or did some other source influence them? At present we are told, in the case of Theseus, that the new imagery responds to the sixth-century epic poem of Theseus' deeds. What epic poem? The evidence for such a text rests solely on the evidence of Athenian vase-painting and the dates currently attributed to its sequence.

Let us judge these questions by looking at the Brygos Painter's Gigantomachy in Berlin (Figs 15, 16, and 17).[88] On the front of the cup, we see Poseidon and Hephaestus fighting back to back against a common foe. On the back of the cup, Athena leads Zeus to the battlefield from his Olympian palace. Crouching behind his father's chariot, Dorian Heracles, dressed as an archer, is almost reluctantly joining the fray, and the battle rages on without him. Poseidon has won his battle, and Hephaestus, with his hammer and tongs, has his adversary very much on the run. In the tondo, we see an image of Selene, newly prominent in this cup, and Michael Vickers and I have tentatively suggested that her action may represent an image of eclipse. In no scene of gigantomachy likely to predate this cup do we see the gods arrayed in such a configuration. The scene is new; does mythical image in this instance replicate history?

Remember, this is an Athenian vase and its manifesto is therefore likely to express an Athenian point of view. At the Battle of Salamis, Athens had staked all her hopes for security on her faith in Poseidon *asphaleios*. Poseidon has already proved his dependability; his battle is won. After Salamis, the Peloponnesians retreated to the Isthmus and tried to make their stand against Xerxes' land army at that strategic point. Athens was outraged, isolated, and her defences thoroughly exposed. Herodotus reports that an eclipse of the sun, a particularly potent omen of divine will, contributed to the Spartans' decision to march north to Plataea and fight together with the Athenians on the Boeotian plain.[89] Thebes, however, the city of Heracles' birth, had thrown in her lot with Persia. The men of Argos, a Peloponnesian state whose mythical associations with Heracles were scarcely less strong, were nowhere to be seen: their government proclaimed a neutral position, but was (and with reason) distrusted as the partisan of Persia. Athens' warrior goddess therefore ensures that both her father and his celebrated son, the hero of Athens' rivals, will arrive in time to save the day. And what of Hephaestus? As the god of smiths, he had presumably forged the gods' armour, as his Athenian craftsmen made the weapons with which their countrymen fought back the Persian invader. More important, however, Hephaestus' cult was virtually restricted to Athens; not only was he the attending obstetrician at Athena's cerebral birth, but also, by her (though superficially so, for she valued her chastity), the father of Erichthonius, the ancestor from whom the Athenians claimed their literal autochthony. Hephaestus is therefore well placed as the representative of Athens' land army.

On this cup, with Salamis won and the Persian land army being driven by Hephaestus from Attic soil, we therefore see the dramatic moment portrayed in Aeschylus' *Persians* when Darius' ghost rises from his grave, lamenting his son's defeat at Salamis and prophesying even greater catastrophe at Plataea:

> So deep shall lie the gory clotted mass
> Of corpses by the Dorian spear transfixed
> Upon Plataea's field! . . . .
> Therefore when ye behold, for deeds like these,
> Such stern requital paid, remember then
> Athens and Hellas.[90]

On a cup by the Painter of the Paris Gigantomachy (Fig. 18),[91] a member of the Brygos Painter's circle and one who elsewhere had the Persians on his mind, we find much the same configuration, but the scene is even more chauvinistically portrayed, for

Poseidon's victory is pre-eminent, Athenian Hephaestus drives away the retreating enemy, and Dionysus the god of epinician symposium contributes to the cause.

3

WORD AND CEREMONY[1]

The deeds of Theseus are a spurre to prowess, and a glasse
How princes' sons and noblemen their youthful days should passe.

These 'lumbering "fourteeners"' are Arthur Golding's, traducing
Ovid in 1565.[2] And this is from Frank Brommer's recent *Theseus*:
'shortly before 510 BC, a cyclic poem about Theseus must have
been composed, for soon afterwards it came to be represented in
vase-painting and in the metopes of the Athenian Treasury.'[3]
Since Felix Jacoby and Karl Schefold argued the case in the
1940s,[4] almost no scholar has seriously questioned 'the exact time
in which [Theseus] became the Athenian hero *par excellence*', to
quote Christiane Sourvinou-Inwood, who goes on to explain why:

> before the last quarter of the sixth century, the position
> occupied by Theseus in Attic art . . . is very modest indeed,
> [but then] there is a sudden change: Theseus representations
> become frequent and are enriched with new episodes . . . . It
> is generally accepted that this change in the popularity of
> Theseus took place under the influence of an epic poem –
> some scholars are in favour of more than one epic poem –
> which created the classical saga definitely annexing Theseus
> to Athens and transforming him into the national hero, the
> model of all high virtues, the achiever of the synoecism and
> of a 'democratised' monarchy, the protector of the people.[5]

Fine sentiments indeed, but let us hear from Eduard Fraenkel,
speaking to the British Academy: 'that fast-growing tenacious
plant, "fable convenue", has crept around the ancient fabric to such
an extent that at many places it completely conceals the old

masonry.' But Professor Fraenkel was not discussing Theophrastus on the *hybris* of plants and so he continues: 'Serious difficulties are persistently avoided or, worse, not even noticed for the sole reason that in the past some influential critic . . . improvised an arbitrary interpretation and handed it down to his successors, who in their turn took the solution for granted.'[6] Fraenkel urges his fellow scholars to

> strive their hardest to disentangle themselves from the fatal
> network of conventionalism and, while taking full advantage
> of the achievements of their forerunners, mercilessly insist on
> the one question: 'what is the evidence?' Not the smallest
> scrap of evidence of any kind should be light-heartedly
> dismissed, but where there is none we should say so, and not
> try to replace it by products of our own fertile imagination.[7]

Now, do we have any documentary evidence which would lead us to reconstruct a sixth-century *Theseid*? As Spencer Barrett pointed out to readers of the *Hippolytus*: 'we knew little enough about this *Theseis* (the three or four references to it merely testify to the existence of such a poem, and imply nothing about its date)',[8] yet he too accepts the lure of precision-dated pottery: 'an epic poem is the obvious vehicle for the building up of a body of legend, and the evidence of the vases makes it reasonable to assign it to the sixth century.'[9] The absence of literary evidence will not detain those who can read a stomach muscle here and a palmette there as if they were date-stamps. I cannot deny that, in broadly defined terms, such stylistic manners may reflect the craftsman's period and his relationships with other artists, but remember, friends of Greek poetry, that in accepting a sixth-century *Theseid* into the corpus of lost cyclic epos, you are relying exclusively on the same folks who, by the application of such criteria, have insisted upon a sixth-century Theseus and Antiope at Eretria which (need I mention it?), together with the Athenian Treasury at Delphi, constitutes the monumental evidence supporting the reconstruction of a sixth-century epic poem. I shall discuss the Athenian Treasury two chapters hence; here suffice it to say that Pausanias (perhaps mistakenly, but nonetheless unambiguously) dates the building after Marathon[10] where I have suggested the Eretrian Amazonomachy may also belong, that no documentary evidence exists which contradicts Pausanias, and that, as John Boardman observes, 'it is a measure of the confidence of scholars in their chronology for archaic Greek art that they are ready to set aside this testimony and prefer an earlier date'.[11]

I return to Sourvinou-Inwood's clear exposition of the evidence for new Thesean iconography: besides the deep-rooted tradition of Theseus' expedition against the Minotaur, she mentions 'Helen's abduction and the Marathon bull, and three [other episodes] of which we cannot find any previous trace in art or literature'; she lists 'the deeds during the journey from Troezen to Athens, Theseus at the bottom of the sea and Theseus and the Amazons.'[12] These three then are all new: the Deeds, the Dive and the Amazons. Now we have seen a Thesean Amazonomachy on what may well be a post-Marathonian gable which, as I argued in the first chapter, could have been built under Cimonian influence in the 470s, the Delphic metopes remain *sub judice*, and we are about to visualize the mural painting of a Thesean Amazonomachy in a building which no one would date before the mid-470s. That same building also displayed a painting of Theseus' Dive, and the same tale is told by Bacchylides in a poem which scholars generally date to the same decade.[13] In extant tradition Bacchylides is also the first to sing of the Deeds, again, so scholars speculate, in the 470s.[14] The dates of these two dithyrambs are tentative and, I readily admit, beyond proof, but students of Bacchylides have long agreed on their plausibility since they accord with other indications suggestive of the poet's activity in Athens during this period. In terms of evidence, image therefore seems to precede extant text (which otherwise precisely matches the image) by a long generation.

Even taking into account the fragmentary record of early Greek poetry, I regard this coincidence of topic and apparent discrepancy of date as striking.[15] Though I cannot deny that a sixth-century epic poem may have provided precedent for Bacchylides' presentation of these Thesean themes, otherwise new in extant Greek poetry, I do not believe that it did, and consider that the basis for confidence in the very existence of such an epic has been overrated. Wilamowitz alone disputed the view that Theseus' new popularity took place under the influence of this epic,[16] but his dissenting voice, though heard, has passed unheeded. Wilamowitz has even been criticized for not arguing his objection, despite the fact that at the time he was discussing Heldensage, not the non-existence of bluebirds. Perhaps he had no idea how 'fast and tenaciously' their perch upon this 'fable convenue' would grow, not least through the assiduous attention of Jacoby. For Jacoby, in a note which has become a touchstone of modern Theseus studies, while declaring that 'the figure of Theseus is in need of a new and unprejudiced treatment . . . cannot follow Wilamowitz (*Heldensage*, 1925 = *Kl. Schr.* v.2, p. 75), who treats this poem as if it were non-existent'.[17] What could be a more proper, 'unprejudiced' way for a philologist to treat a poem that does not exist? But enough of shadowboxing; we have the war-games of the Athenian ephebes to attend.

John Boardman has recently observed 'how readily myth could be adjusted or invented in the service of state, family, or politics.'[18] In this connection, it has become something of a commonplace to recognize that Theseus, 'this other Heracles', as Plutarch called him,[19] came to represent the ambition of Athens' new democracy and the achievements of her leading statesman, Cimon, the son of Miltiades, strategist of Athenian victory at Marathon. I shall speak in the next chapter of the ways in which that victory was elevated to the status of legend and transformed into a memorial to his father, but here my task is to show how Cimon manipulated myth to serve his own political ends by instituting Theseus not only as an Athenian cult hero, but also as his own heroic template. I begin with the shrine Cimon erected to house the hero's remains and decorated with images of his enterprise.

Whenever it occurred – under Cleisthenes, under Cimon – the restoration of Theseus as a hero in whom Athenians could take unambiguous pride cannot have been an altogether easy task. 'Athens', as Joseph Wells once remarked, 'was poorly equipped for an imperial position by legendary greatness.'[20] Before his rape of Antiope, Theseus had only one great international exploit to his credit, his expedition against Crete, to slay the Minotaur. At Troy he played no direct part. Homer speaks of Aethra, his mother, as one of Helen's handmaids, and though his two sons, Acamas and Demophon, are named among the undistinguished Athenian contingent, their leader was the Erechtheid prince, Menestheus, pretender to their father's throne. By contrast with the sons of Aegina, Athens could claim no Iliadic distinction. Moreover, in his quaint account of Theseus' admiration for Heracles – 'by night his dreams were haunted by that hero's deeds, and in the daytime a continual emulation stirred him up to perform the like'[21] – Plutarch at least reflects the tradition that, by the time Theseus laid claim to displace him, Heracles was well established in Athenian cult. The Amazonomachy of Heracles predates Theseus' rape of Antiope, and Theseus' pentathlon on his journey to Athens emulates his cousin's prowess. As Theseus' legends developed, we find him, so to speak, tidying up after Heracles. So when Heracles brought the Cretan bull, Poseidon's gift and father of the Minotaur, back to Eurystheus, it escaped north to the plain of Marathon, ravaging the hamlets of the Tetrapolis until Theseus roped the bull and delivered the local residents from its danger. Later in the century, Athens made increasing political play of the tradition that Theseus had protected the children of Heracles when they sought sanctuary in Attica and opposed Eurystheus' attempt to reclaim them by force of arms. Moreover, though the Athenians claimed their own king, Aegeus, as his mortal father, to Troezenians he was theirs, for Aethra was his mother and they recognized not Aegeus but Poseidon, as his legitimate father. Theseus has thus been born abroad and died in exile, in terms of the later politicizing myth, the first victim of ostracism. So recognizing that a hero needs a ceremonial tomb, Cimon determined to provide one and, by proper burial and cult observance, to reinstate Theseus at the centre of Athenian civic life.

'Myths', writes Martin Nilsson, 'were potent tools in the hands of the clever politician',[22] and so were oracles. Scholars have reasonably speculated that the Alcmaeonids had embellished Apollo's temple at Delphi in exchange for the oracle's support in persuading the Spartans to expel Hippias, the Peisistratid tyrant, thereby establishing Cleisthenes in power. We have already seen how Themistocles' reading of a later oracle was fully vindicated by the outcome of Salamis. We can also observe the political effect of Themistocles' policy which tended to shift the balance of power away from Athens' hoplite army in favour of her newly mobilized marines, the forerunners of the *nautikos okhlos*. Since the fleet was obviously essential for promoting Athens' maritime aspirations thereby opening up vast new sources of wealth, the leaders of her propertied families – in order to resist any infringement of their traditional interests – rather than opposing the navy, chose instead to control it, first through Areistides, hostile to Themistocles since boyhood, and, after a swift apprenticeship, through Cimon.

Cimon's background and personality were well suited to such interests. 'He was more than a fighter of genius; he was a diplomat'[23] possessed, we gather, of unusual charm; Plutarch portrays him as a man aware of the importance of public image and a natural flair for winning popularity. Though too young himself to fight at Marathon, his father's prestige would reflect well upon those who now supported his son and he seems to have been little involved in the political feuding of the 480s. His marriage to Isodice sealed a crucial dynastic bond with the Alcmaeonid clan and, at the beginning of his public career, we see Cimon active on foreign campaigns with Areistides whose patronage he undoubtedly also enjoyed. The coastal fortress of Eion on the Strymon river remained an outpost of Persian defence and, as Joseph Wells has recognized,

> the reduction of Eion was necessary as a defensive measure against a renewed Persian attack . . . [and] as opening up Athenian trade with the interior of Thrace, and as securing for Athens an opportunity for founding those 'Thraceward' settlements which, from the days of Peisistratus onward, had had such an attraction for Athenians.[24]

Under Cimon's generalship the stronghold was encircled and seized. Public acclaim followed this initial success and, at the bidding of the Delphic oracle, Cimon proceeded against the robbers' nest of Scyros. For Cimon, Scyros offered a world of opportunity. The Dolopians who controlled the island had submitted to Xerxes[25] and contributed troops to his infantry,[26] but, in addition to heeding the call for vengeance against those who consorted with the barbarian, Cimon must have recognized that there were more subtle ways in which he could exploit this campaign. This centrally situated island, lying 'in the open sea between Euboea and the islands at the mouth of the Hellespont'[27] could therefore be strategically useful as an Athenian cleruchy commanding the sea-routes to Chalcidice, Lemnos and Thrace where Cimon's father and great-uncle, *oikistes* of the Chersonnese, had already established his family's interests. But we must also understand Cimon's achievement against the background of 'his own rising star, and Themistocles' falling one'. In 476 Themistocles' *choregia* of Phrynichus' *Phoenician Women* evidently brought Themistocles renewed acclaim and Cimon responded with Eion and Scyros, for by liberating the Aegean from the threat of piracy he countered any claim to naval leadership which Themistocles might continue to promote. Moreover, despite murmurs of a rivalry between Themistocles and a local Lycomedes, it would have been easy enough for Cimon to hint at the coincidence between Themistocles' membership of the Athenian Lycomidae and the tradition that Theseus was lured to his death on Scyros by Lycomedes, the island king.

It was time for Cimon to claim Theseus for himself and so, in pious response to the oracle's politically expedient injunction that 'the Athenians should recover the bones of Theseus and watch over them in honour among themselves', Cimon went off in search of appropriately impressive bones. The Invention was guided portentously enough by the bird of Zeus, and Cimon thus came upon a tomb containing the bones of a man of extraordinary, indeed heroic height, and, lying there beside him, a bronze spear and sword.[28] He forthwith translated these remains to Athens 'with pomp and ceremony' where, so Plutarch reports, the hero 'was joyously welcomed by his descendents as if Theseus himself were returning to his city' (*hosper auton epanerkhomenon eis to astu*), and the ceremonies ended with the enshrinement of these bones in the newly erected Theseum. Burial in a prominent part of the city was an honour especially appropriate to the heroic founder of a democratic city (an *heros ktistes* or *oikistes*) and this is how Cimon, Thucydides and Euripides all regarded Theseus.[29]

Let us now look at this Theseum as best we may, for its site is unknown and its paintings are lost. The original site is fraught with controversy but Pausanias situated it 'in the middle of the city by the gymnasium',[30] at a point, so R.E. Wycherley reasonably judges, 'where [he] was leaving the agora in a south-easterly direction'.[31] Such a location, towards the north slope of the Acropolis, would be specially apt once we remember that the Amazons had pitched their tent on Ares' hill as they prepared to attack the Acropolis, 'plotting death for Theseus' and now Theseus rests, Athens' champion, near the site of their repulse, with the image of his victory, so I believe is likely, displayed within his shrine.

I have reconstructed a square shrine *exempli gratia* (Fig. 19), comparing other *heroa*. Though I am not committed to this groundplan I see no reason to share John Barron's 'confidence that the building was in fact rectangular'.[32] Ancient sources variously describe the Theseum as a *temenos*, *sekos*, and a *hieron*.[33] While any of these terms could by itself sufficiently designate the shrine, they need not, as some have thought, exclude each other: *temenos* most commonly denotes a sacred enclosure, and I take *sekos* to refer to the sepulchre itself, the central repository of the Bones, and *hieron*, in Pausanias' usage, to the sanctuary as a whole.

It is Pausanias who supplies our account of the paintings. He mentions three in all: Athenians fighting Amazons, the battle of the Lapiths and Centaurs, and Theseus' reception in Amphitrite's marine palace. It seems likely that Pausanias considered them to be the work of the well-known muralist, Micon. Theseus' presence is explicit in the last two scenes Pausanias describes and it would be perverse to exclude him from an Amazonomachy in his own shrine. Athenians are involved in the battle which may have been a generalized one – for example, on the Marathonian plain – but since Pausanias compares the scene on the Parthenos shield, it is probable that the battle for the Acropolis to which the *Eumenides* later alludes formed at least part of the painting's action (see p. 88). And if we follow T.B.L. Webster's 'glide from the contemporary into the mythical world', we can reconcile with its Thesean precedent the Athenian repulse of the trousered Persians by whom Attica had so recently been invaded.

The *Centauromachy* would have suggested a comparable discourse, one in which Apollonian order triumphs over Dionysian chaos, while perhaps alluding to Cimon's Thessalian connections with Menon of Pharsalus, his own Peirithous. Theseus also dominates the back wall with his dive to the depths of the sea to recover the Ring of Minos. If the scene is comparable with the tale Bacchylides will tell, then he is at the threshold of his reign as his stepmother bestows upon him the tokens which authenticate his rule at sea. As we enter the shrine, we therefore see this image of freshly triumphant youth. And on either side of this coronation Theseus in maturity and now on land conquers his foes at home and abroad.

But what of a fourth painting which has been much in the news this past decade? Many scholars, Martin Robertson among them, have accepted John Barron's defence of such a painting paired with the Ring of Minos and exhibited to its right.[34] The scene of this supposed painting is Theseus in the Underworld and, in Professor Barron's view, a well-known vase-painting – on the Niobid Painter's Louvre crater[35] – reflects the mural. Some might consider this underworld scene as a discreet indication of the hero's exile and death on Scyros from which Cimon had so recently delivered him. Such a pair of paintings would nicely contrast two sons of Zeus, Minos, Theseus' adversary, and Heracles, who brings succour to Theseus. But Pausanias speaks of three paintings and three paintings only. He turns from Micon's *Dive for the Ring of Minos* to recount various and inconsistent legends about the hero's death, but he does not mention the scene represented on the Niobid Painter's crater. I agree with Barron that Jan Six correctly identified the subject of this vase-painting as the dramatic moment when Theseus arose through the intervention of Heracles and Athena from his captivity in Hades. Nonetheless, Pausanias has surely been prompted to his digression on the circumstances of Theseus' death not by the subject of a fourth painting, but by the presence of the sepulchre, the *sekos*, in which the hero's bones reposed.

The idea that vase-paintings may cast 'new light on old walls' is well established, but the illumination frequently issues from marsh lights and the bog can be deep. Even so, Susan Woodford makes an appealing case when she suggests that the Foundry Painter's Munich Centauromachy (Fig. 20)[36] (where Theseus is both central and alone victorious) seems to replicate the second painting Pausanias describes, in which 'Theseus has already killed a centaur, but the rest of the fighting is even'. Dr Woodford herself, however, cannot accept this sensible possibility on the grounds that 'the Foundry Painter's cup is almost certainly earlier than the mural paintings in the Theseion'.[37] She therefore proceeds to reconstruct another 'work of major painting from which it derived – the prototype for the Theseus of the Theseion' which 'was probably destroyed in the Persian sacks of 480 and 479'.[38] When one becomes deft enough to set the chronometer of Attic pottery with such precision, Okham's Razor can be left to rust, for Theseus has yet to do battle with Procrustes.

I would now like to summarize certain features of two Athenian feast days associated with Theseus and celebrated on the seventh and eighth days of Pyanepsion. The seventh of the month was the day specially devoted to Apollo, and the Pyanepsia commemorated the fulfilment of the vows Theseus and his companions had made to the god at Delos when they undertook to honour him with offerings in exchange for their safe return. This then was the day on which Theseus came back to Athens and the religious rites particular to the festival all reflected legendary episodes of his voyage. At the same time, a vintage celebration, known as the Oschophoria, was conducted by the aristocratic Salaminian clan whose ancestors had provided Theseus with his pilot and his lookout man.[39] For it was from Phaleron that the tribute ship had sailed for Crete. To the accompaniment of hymn–singing their procession travelled from a sanctuary of Dionysus in Athens to the Salaminian shrine of Athena Skiras at Phaleron, and there the mothers of the Twice Seven had brought their doomed children bread and meat, and told them tales to cheer them. This ceremony included several unusual features, among them, the presence of female *deipnophoroi*, presumably representing the mothers, who accompanied the procession carrying food for the banquet in which they shared. At the banquet, it was customary for legends to dominate the conversation. One is reminded of the Lesche of the Cnidians at Delphi which R.A. Tomlinson has recently discussed as a *hestiaterion*,[40] a banqueting hall, literally, 'a place to talk', as Pausanias records, 'about traditional myths and more serious matters'.[41] After the 'first fruits had been burnt in honour of Apollo, the banqueters shared the rest of the meat among themselves'; there was no public handout.

On the other hand, things were quite different on the following day, for the eighth of the month was sacred to Poseidon and, on that day, Cimon therefore established the festival of Poseidon's son, Theseus. It is possible that the site of the Theseum previously used by the Phytalidae for some minor worship of the hero was now appropriated by the state for the major new festival. By contrast with the practice of the Oschophoria, the Theseia provided a generous distribution of meat to the populace, one example among many of Cimon's public philanthropy. In this context, we may note H.W. Parke's interesting suggestion that 'it may have been partly an outcome of this general banquet that from the fifth century one can trace a popular belief that Theseus when alive had been a friend of the people and had established a democratic government in his combined state of Athens'.[42]

This festival of Theseus was also a time for athletic competition at first apparently confined to Athenians until metics (resident aliens) were later permitted to enter certain lists. The events themselves seem to have had a 'somewhat military flavour'; we have a record of the festival dating from 161/160 BC, and while it would be unsafe to project the whole programme back three centuries, let me mention some events which might be considered idiosyncratic enough to be original. For example, we hear of prizes for trumpeters and prizes for heralds. Ephebes and *neaniskoi* are prominent in many events, including races in armour; and special prizes for 'manly excellence' and 'good military equipment', like 'races in armour' seem appropriate to the interests of a cadet corps. There is nothing unusual about 'horse races', yet in view of Cimon's early fascination with horses one can understand how such an event might have found a place in a festival he himself had instituted. And we might also mention the long-distance event, the *dolikhos*, which though by no means unique to this festival is again appropriate to the training of a cadet corps among Pheidippides' countrymen.

Pausanias is explicit about the occasion for which this shrine was built[43] and contrasts its relatively recent foundation with that of the Sanctuary of the Dioscuri to which he next turns his attention.[44] So we have a shrine of Theseus and a festival in his honour founded by Cimon in response to an order from Apollo's oracle. With these ideas in mind, let us read two of Bacchylides' dithyrambs to see what light they may shed upon our hero's *aretai* and *erga* and the interests of his earnest patron.

In the last chapter I reflected on the possible ways in which contemporary events might influence both occasional and dramatic poetry. The question of genre is relevant to this discussion: while it would be patently absurd to suggest that Aeschylus composed his *Oresteia* as an aetiology for the reform of the Areopagus, it is indeed the case that certain kinds of poetry may reflect actual ceremonies. Epinician poetry provides one obvious example and, so I shall argue, does Bacchylides' *Dithyramb for the Athenians* (18 Snell). R. Merkelbach has already proposed that an ephebic ceremony provided the specific occasion for its composition.[45] The young Theseus, the *pais prothebos* of lines 56–7 provides an apt mythical archetype for Athenian ephebes who, as Carl Robert suggested long ago, themselves constituted the dramatic chorus of this dithyramb.[46] On the other hand, I disagree with Merkelbach that the dithyramb must postdate 459 when Athens annexed the Megarid and suggest instead that Bacchylides had in mind a much more specifically Athenian occasion, namely the foundation of the Theseum and the festival of the Theseia.

Originally conceived as a hymn to Dionysus, the dithyramb had by classical times for the most part abandoned this restriction of its subject-matter. While this dithyramb of Bacchylides may have 'nothing to do with Dionysus', it alone among extant dithyrambs is composed as a dialogue and as such may reflect one of the most archaic forms of dithyrambic poetry. Let us tentatively accept the tradition that an *hypokrites*, an 'answerer', was introduced to give a distinct, dramatic character to a role formerly taken by the chorus-leader. In Bacchylides' poem, Aegeus (not Medea, as Kenyon first thought)[47] is the *hypokrites* and he is interrogated by the chorus. As Richard Jebb remarks, this dithyramb is not a survival, but a highly developed lyric poem which emulates an archaic model.[48] An archaizing form of this kind could well suit an ephebic occasion, and the language of the ephebic oath itself may perhaps date from the time of the Persian Wars. As P. Siewert has shown, its text also includes several archaic elements,[49] but instead of interpreting this evidence as an indication of the further antiquity of ephebic institutions at Athens, I think such archaism intentionally evoked the deep-rooted conservative tradition which reflected the social backgrounds of candidates for what was in effect a corps of cadets.

To return to Bacchylides' poem: the chorus of ephebes asks the king why he has sounded the trumpet-call to arms. Is their country threatened by external invasion, or has he been aroused by some inner anxiety? The king replies: a herald has just returned from the long road (*dolikhan*) to the Isthmus bringing news of unspeakable feats by a man of power, feats which Aegeus proceeds to enumerate. The chorus then inquire the identity and origin of this man: does he come at the head of an army, or walk alone with attendants, wandering to a foreign land (*alatan* often denotes a roaming exile while *ep' allodamian* implies foreign residence)? The irony resounds: the anonymous stranger is no mere adventurer seeking refuge in Attica, but Aegeus' own son who, having come of age, now advances upon Athens to claim his inheritance. In the final strophe Aegeus answers these questions as he reports the herald's news: 'Two men alone accompany him, and round his splendid shoulders he has a sword with an ivory hilt. Two polished spears are in his hands and a well-fashioned Laconian hat upon his head of burnished hair; he wears a purple *chiton* round his chest and a Thessalian *chlamys* [described as *oulios*]. From his eyes flashes a Lemnian flame. He is a youth in first manhood mindful of the games of Ares and the clashing bronze of battle. And he seeks out Athens, lover of *aglaia*, brilliant celebration.'

A trumpet-blast, a herald, the wargames of the ephebic *hoplitodromoi*: can we hear an echo of the festival of Theseus I described a few moments ago? At any rate, Merkelbach is surely correct in his view that, although neither Aegeus nor the chorus is yet aware of his identity, Theseus' companions may well represent two ephebes who, true to their custom, have come from patrolling the border as a pair. The herald has given Aegeus a telling account of his son's distinguishing marks which, despite the *xiphos* at line 48, recall not so much the traditionally simple *gnorismata* of the Troezenian's hero's sandals and sword, but, taken together with the *chlamys*, the equipment of an Athenian ephebe, and more pointedly, when we add to the distinctive sword the stranger's 'polished spears', we are reminded of Theseus' Scyrian grave goods.[50]

If Bacchylides composed his *Dithyramb for the Athenians* to accompany the 'pomp and ceremony' attendant upon the foundation of the Theseum and the Return of the Bones, then can we discover anything of the hero's Athenian patron in the language of this ode? From the lurid traditions of Cimon's reported progeny, John Davies accepts the names of three sons as certain, Thettalos, Oulios and his twin Lakedaimonios,[51] and, following John Barron's lead,[52] we may notice how cunningly Bacchylides has woven these names into the fabric of his final strophe:

50   *keutukton kunean Lakai–*
                 nan kratos peri pursokhaitou.
             khitona porphureon
             sternois t'amphi, kai oulion
             Thessalan khlamud'. ommaton de
55   *stilbein apo Lamnian*
             phoinissan phloga.

In lines 50–1 a topographical epithet follows the adjective/noun phrase (*keutukton kunean* + *lakainan*). At the end of the description, this arrangement is reversed (*Lamnian* + *phoinissan phloga*) while in lines 53–4, the place-name *Thessalan* divides adjective from noun.

Let us look at these phrases more closely, beginning with the Thessalian *chlamys*. I have referred to the *chlamys* as 'ephebic', but mention of Thessaly may also allude to Theseus' traditional friendship with Peirithous, the Lapith King whom Theseus succoured in the conflict against the centaurs. This mythical alliance may be seen to prefigure an historical one which Cimon formed with Menon of Pharsalus who provided both money and cavalry in support of Cimon's campaign at Eion. Even if shortly

55

before his ostracism, Cimon tried to repudiate his Thessalian proxeny, he had already named a son Thettalos, and by doing so, A.E. Raubitschek has argued, commemorated this connection with his Pharsalian ally.[53] Plutarch moreover reports that Cimon's first intervention on Scyros had been provoked by a gang of Dolopian pirates. The practical and mythical connotations of the Thessalian *chlamys* thus converge with significant events in Cimon's personal and public life.

The adjective *oulion* tells a similar story. I am unpersuaded by Barron's argument that here alone in Greek, *oulion* means *oulan* 'woolly, thick'.[54] The fibre content of a Thessalian chlamys seems of scant importance when we remember that, in Attic vase-painting, the sight of Theseus dressed in a chlamys and wreaking vengeance on the villains he encounters during his Saronic progress is a thoroughly familiar one. Theseus' garment is indeed with justice called *oulios*, 'deadly', and we may recall Pherecydes' report, unknown from any other source, that Theseus made sacrifice to Apollo Oulios and Artemis Oulia before departing for Crete.[55]

Oulios, as we have noticed, is also the name of one of Cimon's sons, and it may have been during the 470s that Pherecydes enrolled an Oulios in his extraordinary genealogy of Cimon's ancestors (Fig. 21).[56] Notice how Pherecydes has coopted for Athens the Aeginetan heroes Telamon and Ajax whom we met in Chapter 2, and derives Cimon's house from that hoary Salaminian, Cynchreus, who along with the Aeacids had made himself manifest at the great sea-battle, just as Theseus himself at Marathon 'had rushed in full armour leading the Athenian charge against the barbarian'.[57] We have already noticed the strong Salaminian connection with Theseus' cult and Pherecydes has cleverly found a way of authenticating it in Cimon's favour. But Pherecydes' service to Cimonian polity went further, for we see that Oulios' father is Agenor 'leader of men'. This relationship between an Agenor and an Oulios deep in Philaid ancestry provides a remarkable commentary on Cimon's own aspirations, for, according to this genealogical fiction, Cimon as the father of a second Oulios asserts that he himself is a new 'leader of men'. Such manipulation of mythology in the service of dynastic ambition is a familiar game which, as Herodotus reports, the Peisistratids had already played with skill.[58]

Like the *chlamys*, a 'well-made Laconian *kunee*' – whether the headgear in question is a cap or a *petasos*[59] – is a common attribute of Theseus on Athenian vases. *En men oun ap' arkhes philolakon*, Plutarch writes of Cimon,[60] and Cimon's philolaconian tendency scarcely requires comment. For us it is enough to notice that Oulios' twin was called Lakedaimonios and that the compass points indicated by Thessaly, Sparta and Lemnos have both a pan-Hellenic and, for Cimon, a personal resonance.

In its proverbial sense, the phrase 'Lemnian fire' aptly characterizes the ferocity of Theseus' glance and matches the devastating connotations of *oulion*. From a topographical standpoint, however, Lemnos belongs no less to Cimon's own career since the island lies directly on the sea-route from Athens to Eion and Byzantium. Its mention may therefore recall Cimon's campaigns in the northern Aegean following Mycale, and also his father's colonization of the island with Athenian settlers at the beginning of the century. The fact that the Lemnian volcano of Moschylos was sacred to Hephaestus may not be without significance to students of contemporary gigantomachies. And so, after celebrating the future generation of Cimon's sons, Bacchylides now turns the present to the past by invoking a significant point of contact between Cimon's own career and that of Miltiades his father. Those who find these allusions pedantically inappropriate for their Alexandrianism should remember that contemporary painters like Polygnotus found no difficulty in representing Cimon's sister, Elpinice, as Laodice, Priam's captive daughter, who survived the Sack of Troy to become the mother of Mounychos, eponymous ancestor of Attic Mounychion, by one of Theseus' sons who after the war had settled in Thrace.[61] John Barron has good reason to conclude that 'at the climax of the poem, Bakchylides' description of Theseus seems to contain allusions to Kimon's father [and mother], and to all three of his sons. If rightly recognized, their message must be that Kimon is a second Theseus.'[62]

At the end of the dithyramb the poet reveals the warrior's destination: he comes in search of Athens and so the goal of his quest rings back to the chorus' opening invocation of 'sacred Athens' king'. *Philoglaous Athanas: aglaia* is typically used in *epinician* poetry of 'gracious celebration' and we already know which celebration Bacchylides has so adroitly enacted. The premonitions of the first three strophes are thus fulfilled in the last when myth and history come together. The warrior, accompanied by ephebes, is about to arrive in Athens from exploits of glorious achievement, recalling the wresting of Salamis from Sciron's

57

Megarid and, closer to home, Athens' early annexation of Eleusis, Cercyon's wrestling-ground.

Theseus comes from Troezen, where the Athenians and their gods sought sanctuary from the Persians, so Professor Hammond has recently argued, in September of 481,[63] and where they stayed until Athens had been made safe for their return. Under the protection of divinity Theseus is presented to us both as ideal ephebe (line 56) and, by this 'purple *chiton*' in line 52, as ideal marine. This is the hero whom Cimon sees as his own mythical avatar. Theseus is about to be acknowledged by Aegeus, his father; Cimon will carry on the heroic colonialism of his own father, Miltiades. Just as Theseus has outlawed brigandage on land, clearing the corridor between Athens and the Peloponnese, so Cimon, himself a naval commander at Salamis, has now wrought vengeance on the Aegean pirates and promises, in Theseus' name, to cut his own Procrustes down to size. At line 42, the Chorus' commentary on Theseus' action in 'devising just punishment for the unjust' adumbrates Cimon's policy as he leads Delian allies in their just war against the Persian oppressor and his quislings. So even if Bacchylides' dithyramb was not performed at the actual occasion of the Return of Theseus' bones to Athens, at least we may, I think, be confident that he composed it to commemorate that event.

And here perhaps we may see, on a fragmentary *skyphos* in the Louvre,[64] the dénouement of the ceremony I have been attempting to reconstruct. Aegeus wears a wreath; could it be in his role as the *hypokrites* of our dithyramb? On one side of the *skyphos*, the Brygos Painter has depicted a selection of Theseus' exploits on his long road from Troezen to Athens: from left to right, Sinis, the Sow with Phaia and, under the handle, Eleusinian Cercyon. Theseus' sword, his typical *gnorisma*, is visible in the background above them and his *chiton* (which, so Michael Vickers reasonably suggests, reflects the uniform of an Athenian marine) is slung over the olive tree that links the scenes on the front and the back of the vase. As Bacchylides' poem ends, Theseus' advent is at hand; on the vase, the journey is complete as Aegeus greets his son.

Let us now consider Bacchylides' other Theseus dithyramb,[65] which describes the hero's authentication as overlord of the sea. To understand the message of this poem we should resist the current fashion of reading it as an extended metaphor for what C.P. Segal has called 'Theseus' symbolical initiation into . . . the mysteries of mature sexuality'.[66] Segal cites with evident approval Gregory Nagy's view that Sappho's watery plunge from the Leucadian Rock is connected with 'the sexual act and the feeling of lassitude or deathlike feeling which follows it'.[67] For Segal, lovers' plunges come in two varieties, a plunge from a cliff or a plunge of a more intimately erotic kind, but

> in both aspects of the plunge the hero touches the mysteries
> of existence. In both aspects too he passes through a death-
> like point of transition on his way to rebirth, a transition
> which forms the boundary between consciousness and
> unconsciousness, vitality and stupor, waking and sleep,
> darkness and light. . . . The political side of the struggle
> between the two kings [sic!], however, receives relatively
> little emphasis in Bacchylides' account.[68]

While we may agree that the poet's attention to the contrast between unbridled lust and formally acknowledged marriage is a significant one, many will feel justifiably ill at ease within the aura of such closet Freudianism[69] and so we shall leave any sexual aspects of Theseus' plunging to Dr Segal's Misty Beethovenian couch. I shall instead dwell on just those political aspects of the poems which Segal has so undervalued.

At least in retrospect, these two Theseus dithyrambs form a narrative pair. One commemorates Theseus' territorial rites of passage while the second records his sea-victory over Minos. The fact that one of the murals of Cimonian Theseum and also Bacchylides' dithyramb both narrate Theseus' naval victory and his coronation by Amphitrite provides an important point of contact between the painting and the poem, so much so that we are reminded of the observation attributed to Bacchylides' uncle, Simonides, to the effect that 'painting is silent poetry, and poetry speaking painting'.[70] This is Pausanias' description of the painting:

> To anyone unacquainted with legend the painting on the
> third wall is confused, partly through time, and partly
> because Micon has not painted the whole story. As Minos
> brought Theseus to Crete with a shipload of boys and girls,
> he fell in love with Periboea, but Theseus strongly resisted
> this [and as we glance again at the point at which Theseus
> entered Cimon's family tree (Fig. 21), we can see why].

Minos flung many angry taunts at Theseus, including this:
Theseus was no son of Poseidon because he could not recover
the signet ring Minos was wearing, if Minos dropped it into
the sea. With these words, Minos dropped the ring and the
story goes that when Theseus came out of the water he had
the ring and golden wreath, a present from Amphitrite.[71]

This in prosaic terms is the gist of Bacchylides' narrative, with one
crucial omission, namely, the scene in which Theseus came into
Amphitrite's presence and received these tokens of authority. The
passage is omitted for the obvious reason that Pausanias had no
reason to describe it, for that was the subject of the painting he
saw, and all he felt required to do was put this unfamiliar scene in
its narrative context.

Figures 22–24 show a cup in New York by the Briseis Painter, a
member of the Brygan circle.[72] On the front (Fig. 22) we see
Theseus and Athena in her temple. On the back (Fig. 23), the hero
is in the court of his divine father, Poseidon, and Amphitrite, his
stepmother. Thus the two deities most influential in the history of
Attica unite in their patronage of the greatest of all Athenian
heroes. The scene in the tondo (Fig. 24) stands in sharp contrast to
the experience of Theseus' Dorian counterpart, Heracles. Instead of
suffering a jealous Hera's wrath, the young Theseus is graciously
welcomed by his marine stepmother who bestows upon him tokens
of sovereignty and prestige. The front of the cup is a departure
scene in which Athena's outstretched arm directs Theseus towards
his new task. On the outside of the cup we are looking at the
mothers of the Twice Seven at the Oschophoria and notice on the
left, just outside the temple, the woman standing with her arms
raised in consternation as she foresees the dangers he will face.

Bacchylides' dithyramb begins in a similar manner. The first
word, 'dark-prowed', as Adam Parry well said, 'stands . . . at the
prow of his poem, and is used to give the right sinister tone to the
voyage to Crete'.[73] Bacchylides then recounts the tale of Theseus'
journey with the tribute ship carrying the seven youths and seven
maidens as sacrificial victims to Minos. Even the sail of the ship is
called 'a shroud which can be seen from afar' (line 5), which not
only continues the mood of foreboding, but foreshadows the tragic
outcome of Theseus' return to Athens. The story Bacchylides tells,
however, is transformed from one of dread to one of bright joy,
and our cup follows the same progress.

So too, the myth which Bacchylides and the Briseis Painter relate, along with other Athenian paintings of the early fifth century, not least Micon's mural in the Theseum, seems to be new at this period. Theseus' encounter with Minos now takes place, not in the underground of a Cretan labyrinth, but in Poseidon's sea, an element of which Minos arrogantly claims to be lord. Minos, with his insatiate lust, the son of a Phoenician,[74] is portrayed by Bacchylides as steering a wild course of passion, while Athenian Theseus keeps his ship on the sea-paths of justice. This encounter between two cousins is by no means necessarily in mere preparation for Theseus' duel with the Minotaur. It is enough for Athenian Theseus to prove himself the true son of Poseidon, and through his simple piety be recognized by the denizens of the sea as the mortal lord of their realm. Zeus promptly answers his son's appeal, and Minos in premature triumph casts his ring into the deep, ordering Theseus to retrieve it if he can. His companions fear all hope is lost and Theseus leaps into the sea amid their general lamentation. As the Dionysian part of this dithyramb draws to its close, dolphins escort Theseus to his father's house, and we shall presently see them in the tondo of Onesimos' Louvre cup (Fig. 25),[75] where Triton supports his half-brother in the presence of both Amphitrite and Athena. On the back of Briseis Painter's cup (Fig. 23), Triton cuts an impressive figure as he prepares to take Theseus inside the underwater mansion. It is interesting to note that the painter and Bacchylides agree in their portrayal of the two Nereids who welcome Theseus on the left of the scene, for 'fillets interwoven with gold encircle their hair' (lines 105–6).

The climax of Bacchylides' song is likewise seen in the tondo of our cup. Theseus and Amphitrite are now alone, as Theseus stands before his stepmother to receive her gifts, and the gifts are those which Bacchylides describes. Theseus wears the mantle, appropriately *porphyrean* (line 112), and is about to receive her next gift, a 'blameless wreath' (line 114). Thus clad, Theseus reappeared by his ship 'unwetted out of the sea, a miracle to everyone and the gifts of gods shone around his limbs' (lines 123–4). The warlord of Cnossus has met his match. The Nereids rejoice, and the youths and maidens raise a victory paean as the world of Dionysus yields to one of Apollonian order. Bacchylides calls the garment which Amphitrite wraps around her stepson at line 112 an *aion*, which Kurt Latte has plausibly interpreted as an Egyptian loan-word denoting luxurious fabric.[76] The mantle Theseus wears in the

Briseis Painter's tondo (Fig. 23) could well be so described, but this investiture may have a more specific point. The typical mantle of an ephebe was the *chlamys*, but in all three scenes of the Briseis Painter's cup, Theseus wears the costume of the marine. In the tondo, he now receives the purple garment which thus becomes as much a token of his new maritime authority as his *chlamys* signified his ephebic office.

John Barron, however, has with great ingenuity seen in *aion*, the name of Theseus' garment, an allusion to Cimon's recent victory at Strymonian Eion, 'empurpled with the blood of Boges and the Persian garrison whom Kimon annihilated'.[77] This intriguing suggestion gains plausibility when we remember that, in the Lesche of the Cnidians at Delphi, Polygnotus painted a Trojan with the otherwise unknown name of Eioneus, the 'man of Eion'.[78] As Barron remarks, 'implicit in the invention of these names is a view of the Persian War as analogous to the Trojan, and of Kimon's victory at Eion as comparable with the Sack of Troy. It is a comparison made explicit in the victory epigrams to be seen on the Hermai in the Agora at Athens.'[79]

Minos sent Theseus diving to the depths of the sea to seek his ring, a ring that recalls Herodotus' tale of Polycrates and his place in history as the first lord of a maritime empire since the days of Minos.[80] While Pausanias (perhaps forgetfully) refers to this ring, it is, so far as I know, neither recorded by Athenian painters nor does Bacchylides' Theseus return it. Theseus' paternity is authenticated and his new authority manifest by his cloak and his wreath. The wreath – this Cycladic wreath – proclaims his victory and magnificently symbolizes his superiority over Minos. The Minoan (indeed, the Phoenician) mastery of the seas belongs to the past: under the leadership of Theseus with Athena and Poseidon as his patrons, Athens now rules the waves.

Bacchylides' dithyramb is surely a manifesto for the Delian League. This proposal seems justified on several grounds. The poem celebrates the naval exploits of the Athenian Theseus, and as it opens, Athena, armed with her aegis causes the North Wind to fill the ship's sails, driving it towards its goal. Once Theseus' story has been told, a paean is sung and the poet invokes Delian Apollo, praying that he will grant a god-sent fortune of blessings. The message is clear: the role of Athens as a just saviour deserves the attention of a Cean chorus directing its pious praise to Delian Apollo. The Delian League has been formed among Athens' allies, especially her Ionian allies, to protect Greece against invasion 'until iron shall float'. I suggested in the last chapter that an allusion to a contemporary event may be signalled by a significant change in iconographic convention. From this standpoint, the naval encounter between Theseus and Minos presents a new alternative to the traditional story of the labyrinth, and the introduction of such a variant can, I think, best be understood as the product of a political faction striving to promote the role of Theseus as a naval commodore with divine rights to sail the seas.

By characterizing Theseus as the founder of democratic institutions he himself sought both to serve and to control, Cimon had outwitted Themistocles in political strategy as, in a comparison of their respective, social talents, he is also reputed to have sung *dexioteron* than his rival.[81] The youthful Theseus of either dithyramb or cup could provide an appealing model for the young son of Miltiades who led a squadron of Athenian marines to victory at Salamis, and who proceeded to serve his city as admiral in the formative years of the Delian League. Athens, victorious against the Persians by both land and sea, finally wrought with her proud new fleet an association between the domains of Athena and Poseidon who had in myth so long contested her rule. Theseus, her brave young leader – the son of one and the protégé of the other – had single-handedly achieved this agreeable rapprochement. By pointed contrast to Hera's treatment of Heracles, Theseus' stepmother receives him graciously. In these terms we can readily appreciate how appropriate was such an image (Fig. 25) as the chief decoration of Theseus' new shrine, symbolizing as it did divinely sanctioned hegemony. Theseus' career was thus supported by his stepmother, not (as in Heracles' case) opposed by her enmity.[82]

Bacchylides was a native son of Ceos and proud of his heritage. Let me briefly mention his island's major temple, the temple of Athena at Carthaea.[83] The decorative remains of this temple are very fragmentary, but the base of one acroterion is inscribed with the name of Theseus, the central acroterion is a Victory, and Antiope may also be present – or could she not be an Amphitrite? Ceos was an early member of the Delian League and – I think the point may be significant – with traditionally close ties to Eretria. A new temple of Athena including Theseus in its decoration would fit well with Cimonian aspirations for the Delian League and parallel similar developments at Eretria. Bacchylides' marine dithyramb acknowledges Theseus' righteous hegemony and closes with a prayer that Delian Apollo will be 'cheered by choruses of Ceans and bestow on them a fortune of fair blessings'. Where and why was it sung? The simplest answer would be, like Pindar's fourth *Paean*, by Ceans on Delos, perhaps in connection with the foundation of their new temple of Athena. But I am haunted by the strange ceremonies of the Oschophoria which, on Apollo's feast-day, proceeded from a sanctuary of Dionysus to the Salaminian shrine of Athena, replicating the departure of the Twice Seven and offering thanksgiving for their deliverance in fulfilment of vows contracted on Delos. The procession and the feast heard the chant of hymns telling the legend of Theseus,[84] and the Cean choir at the poem's close may simply ring in another self-reflective signature by our Cean nightingale.

Within the political conditions of the middle 470s to early 460s I would set both Bacchylides' dithyramb and the Briseis Painter's cup. Indeed, is it likely that a scene which emphasizes Theseus' reception by Amphitrite could be developed during a period that preceded the formation of Athens' naval enterprise?[85] It is not enough to suppose that Greek myths were conceived at random. We should be discontent with the hypothesis that a poet or painter could have represented Theseus' reception by Amphitrite at any period of Athenian history according to an iconographic imagination disconnected from the culture in which he lived. We can be sure that in the fifth century the narrative of Theseus' myth was manipulated for political ends. It seems much more likely that contemporary events informed the telling of Theseus' tale rather than that 'a pretty picture' was devised in a cultural vacuum. Let us at least entertain the hypothesis that the tondo of Onesimos' Louvre cup (Fig. 25) in which Athena formally introduces Theseus to Amphitrite – indeed, the decorative programme of that cup taken as a whole – belongs to the same cultural background I have just described and expresses a comparable manifesto.

As John Boardman has so well expressed it in a passage from which I have quoted before,

> the attempt to trace and date [innovations in iconography
> and myth] is sometimes tantalizingly imprecise, but the
> search helps to demonstrate how readily myth could be
> adjusted or invented in the service of state, family or politics.
> It is a factor in the development of Greek myth which is

seriously underestimated by those who hope to find in it, as in the mythologies of other cultures, deep and primeval truths about man and his view of his place in the world.[86]

I do not claim to have introduced new and definitive criteria for reinterpreting the chronology of all Greek pottery, but I do suggest that the discrepancies between hypothesis and extant evidence to which I have tried to draw attention deserve reconsideration according to the terms I have proposed. There are surprisingly few shrines in Attica which are dedicated to Theseus – Philochorus mentions only four – and as Parke has suggested, 'the cult before Cimon's political move had probably been in the hands of a few aristocratic families who claimed descent from those who had accompanied Theseus to Crete'.[87] In this context we perhaps think in particular of the Salaminioi, but we must not forget the Phytalidai[88] because they belonged to the deme of Lakiadai, and so did Cimon.

I do not deny that Cleisthenes was also closely associated with Theseus and, as synoecist, the myth suited the Alcmaeonid reformer. But the evidence for this tradition can be most readily understood in the period immediately postdating Cimon's death, when new claims arise for the inheritance of Theseus' mantle and mythological revisionists once again set to work to rewrite history. As L.H. Jeffery has remarked, 'Theseus' epic career appears to have reached its final shape and popularity in the second quarter of the fifth century as a justification for Empire building'.[89] And so we see Cimon as the Alcmaeonids' protégé, standing behind the banner of Theseus as the hero of battles on land and at sea. At the end of the next decade, events would turn against Cimon and he found himself driven from Athens by political factions urged on by Pericles, the son of the man who had, a generation earlier, impeached Cimon's own father, Miltiades. But, for the moment, Cimon, like Theseus, has freed the Aegean; like Cimon, he is a young and pious man, keeping his ship of state 'in the sea-paths of justice'. On his initial reception at Athens, Theseus will drive Medea and her son Medus, whom Aeschylus' Darius names as the ancestor of the Medes and Persians,[90] away from Attic soil, an action which did not pass unnoticed by Athenian vase-painters.[91] And now, with Cimon at the helm, Athens and her Delian allies have the authority to control the Aegean and keep it free of all oppressors. The whole conception of this mythical ideology seems brilliantly contrived to promote the political aspirations of one man, this other Theseus, Cimon himself.

'Cimon was a true aristocrat in the sense given to the word by Aristotle'[92] and he had done his task well. In the second century of our era when another great philanthropist, Herodes Atticus, aspired to touch such intimations of grandeur and prestige, he not only claimed descent from Cimon, Miltiades and Theseus according to the Aeacid genealogy Pherecydes had concocted for Cimon, but he chose Elpinice as his own daughter's name.[93] And when, in the same century, Hadrian built his ornate arch with its elegant superstructure of Corinthian columns as a massive gateway to the city's most venerable remains, the inscription carved on its western frieze proclaimed: 'This is Athens, the ancient city of Theseus.'[94]

In the next chapter I shall take you across the Agora to inspect another Cimonian memorial, the most remarkable of them all. We have seen a room with a tomb; in the next chapter we shall look at a tomb with a view.

4

'SILENT POETRY'

In the last chapter we laid a hero to rest in a tomb decorated with scenes of his enterprise on land and sea. We buried Theseus as the 'founding hero' of Athenian democracy and listened to Bacchylides celebrate the Return of the True Bones and the festival instituted to commemorate this occasion, befitting the hero no less than Patroclus' Funeral Games upon the plain of Troy. 'The Athenian Empire in the Aegean was thus consecrated'[1] and while Wells reminds us of the Translation of St Mark's relics from Alexandria to Venice, Pausanias makes a point of comparing the Spartans' Invention and Return of the bones of Orestes in the previous century, and likewise at Delphi's behest.[2] In this chapter, I shall take you from the shrine probably built on the ground from which Amazon and Persian invaders had assaulted the Athenian Acropolis to one which presented to its beholders the view from a tomb some twenty-six miles to the northeast. The monument was not constructed merely as a 'praise of time past', but in order to concentrate public attention upon recent acts of communal heroism and, in particular, to glorify the role of Cimon's father in devising the victory from which all of Athens' subsequent glories derived. Its decoration may thus reflect Cimon's wish to idealize the hoplites of Marathon at the expense of Themistocles' naval triumphs at Artemisium and Salamis. And, though the Stoa Poikile was not itself by any means a tomb, its programme can be associated with other important developments in Athenian public life which many would date to the period of its construction, or shortly before. I think in particular of the provision of a public cemetery to honour the casualties of the Wars of Empire, and the introduction of the 'Speech at the Tomb' to dedicate to memory their sacrifice and place the campaigns on which they died in the honour roll of battles past, thereby imbuing them with the immortality of heroism.

In the last chapter I mentioned a few of the early skirmishes which characterized Athens' factionalized politics from the expulsion of Hippias and throughout the fifth century. Miltiades' family had long been rivals of the Alcmaeonids at home and abroad so it is not surprising that Xanthippus as a member of that family not only prosecuted Miltiades in the year following Marathon, but shortly afterwards, joined his own kin as an early victim of ostracism. In the 470s the Alcmaeonids rallied round Themistocles' old rival, Aristeides, field-general at the battle of Plataea, and seem to have eulogized his contribution to victory at Salamis, maybe overestimating his role in order to diminish Themistocles'. And they married Isodice to their own protégé, Cimon (who was also said to have seen distinguished service at Salamis),[3] though it appears that he and Pericles, son of Xanthippus, continued their fathers' animosity towards each other. From the start, Cimon's partisans worked against Themistocles, and if one may place any credibility in Pausanias' report that Delphi 'refused the dedication of Persian spoils from Themistocles alone',[4] one suspects Alcmaeonid intrigue, for their influence at the shrine had long been considerable and had been scarcely undermined by Themistocles' coup in the matter of the 'wooden walls'. Nonetheless, at Athens, it had been Aristeides who was ostracized in the 480s, but the continued infighting of the next decade was in the end too much for Themistocles, and by 470 he had left the city for good.

Symbols had come to play an important part in the propaganda battles of these post-war years and it will be instructive to review some of them in summary. The distortion of the Tyrannicide legend which Thucydides[5] was at such pains to correct can plausibly be seen to owe its patent revisionism to the conflicting claims of Athens' main factions. The Parian Marble[6] records that new statues of Harmodius and Aristogeiton were set up in 477/6 to replace Antenor's earlier bronze monument which the Persians had robbed. In general terms the manifesto of this new monument is plain enough: in our father's generation, we threw out our own tyrants; now we have defeated the tyrants of the world whom Hippias himself had urged to reinstate Peisistratid rule. But who in fact deserved the legitimate credit for this achievement? Was it the Alcmaeonids and their Spartan allies, or, as Themistocles' supporters counterclaimed,[7] the two men that had slain the tyrant's brother and so found themselves transformed from beleaguered lovers to political visionaries who, by championing the revolution for liberty, had sacrificed their lives to usher in the new democratic age? The dubious historicity of such a portrait did not pass unnoticed: K.H.Kinzl has recently interpreted the somewhat droopy pair on a vase in Boston (Fig. 26)[8] as a parody of the Tyrannicides' stalwart pose and Hyperides[9] cites a law which forbids the maligning of Harmodius and Areistogeiton 'presumably enacted', as P.J. Rhodes suggests, 'because such attacks were being made'.[10]

Cimon responded to the challenge with characteristic flair. His expedition to Scyros, sanctioned by Apollo, was in the event a fitting response to Themistocles' shrewd decipherment of Aristonice's delphic utterance, but Themistocles' patronage of Phrynichus, and his friendship with Simonides, still provided him with influential spokesmen. Cimon replied, as we have seen, through Pherecydes and Bacchylides and, though somewhat later, Ion of Chios. When the Persians burned the telesterion of the Lycomidae at Phlya, Themistocles, a member of the genos, rebuilt it at his own expense and decorated it with paintings, and Plutarch reports that Simonides celebrated its rededication.[11] If Plutarch's tradition is correct, then Themistocles' action calls into question either the authenticity of the Oath of Plataea or the effective enforcement of its authority. At any rate, Cimon's Shrine of Theseus erected in the heart of Athens eclipsed his rival's dedication and, though its murals are lost, we may yet be able to glimpse something of the finesse by which Cimon appropriated the contemporary preoccupation with the Tyrannicide legend for himself.

While accepting John Boardman's wise caution against the danger of using vase-paintings to reconstruct lost murals,[12] I am attracted by John Barron's speculation that the central images of the two paintings on the side-walls of the Theseum (the Amazonomachy and the Centauromachy) may contain reflections of the Tyrannicide poses.[13] Barron writes of 'the sense of urgency . . . imparted to the scene by the device of the back-to-back pair, springing apart against the enemy'.[14] We have already seen this

69

'device' no less clearly in the Berlin Gigantomachy (Fig. 15) where a comparable, 'Tyrannicide' manifesto would certainly be appropriate. On the other hand, when Barron declares that 'our murals of *c. 475 disclose* [my italics] that these statues at once became the favoured model for violent, warlike action',[15] he surely overstates the evidence, albeit with Jacobian precedent. Nonetheless, if we are entitled to estimate that Theseus as the protagonist of both Amazonomachy and Centauromachy was represented in the likeness of a tyrannicide, then we can understand how skilfully Cimon exploited this imagery to characterize his own heroic ancestor, Theseus, as the archetypal tyrant-slayer.

If then we are to see Theseus with his Thessalian friend Peirithous 'fighting back to back' [or 'side by side'] as later in the Centauromachy on the west pediment at Olympia, we may recognize not only an association with Homeric precedent, but perhaps also an attempt, motivated by his own friendship with Menon, to exorcize the recent memory of Thessaly's medism.[16] At the same time, however, we may even see, from the standpoint of the Tyrannicides, a reminder of Hippias' successful repulse of Anchimolius' liberating army when the tyrant had received timely aid from Cineas' Thessalian cavalry, centaurs indeed. Later in the fifth century, artists like the Kodros Painter[17] exploited the image of Theseus with the tyrannicide's mantle in response to new political circumstances similarly reflected in the decoration of the Hephaesteum.

In the last chapter, I suggested reasons which encourage me at least to entertain the possibility that the scene in the tondo of Onesimos' Louvre cup (Fig. 24) reflects, at least in general terms, the subject of the painting which occupied the rear wall of Cimon's Theseum, facing the entrance to the shrine. In Onesimos' tondo we see Theseus in a marine landscape no less appropriate for an interior scene than Dionysus' boat in Exekias' Munich cup:[18] there, a vessel floating in a wine-dark sea, and here, our hero in the underwater court of his stepmother, Poseidon's queen. And as is the case of the battle scenes of Exekias' cup, Onesimos has decorated the outside with deeds performed on dry land. So too, in the Theseum itself, the central image of the decorative programme is surrounded on either side with scenes of Theseus' enterprise on land.

In discussing the development of Theseus' legend, I also pointed out the striking and relatively consistent discrepancy between the likely dates of the first texts which relate the Deeds and the Dive, and the period at which the first images of these new scenes are usually thought to have been introduced. Though I realize it is a proverb of hell, I take heart from William Blake's observation that 'the road of excess leads to the palace of wisdom' and accordingly progress from this palace of Amphitrite to a pair of well-known images with which Myson decorated an amphora, now also in the Louvre (Figs 27 and 28).[19] Of this vase and its artist, John Boardman writes as follows:

> Myson was not an artist of notable iconographical
> imagination, and the vase was surely a special commission. It
> couples a unique memorial to pious Kroisos at the moment of
> his downfall, with a mythological scene, a version of which
> was to be used to reflect upon an Athenian enterprise against
> the new lords of Kroisos' capital. On a special vase, such as
> this, juxtaposition is unlikely to be accidental.[20]

'Pious Kroisos': *ou phthinei Kroisou philophron areta*. The quotation comes from the end of Pindar's first Pythian composed to celebrate Hiero's victory at Delphi in the chariot race of 470, but two years later, when the Syracusan tyrant won the most prestigious of all events, the chariot race at Olympia, it was Bacchylides whom he commissioned to celebrate his victory. Bacchylides also sang of Croesus, capping Pindar.[21]

In Bacchylides' ode, Croesus' philanthropy to Delphi is duly acknowledged and, at the moment of his downfall, both Apollo and Zeus intervene to reward his *eusebeia*. As Cyrus' army begins to sack the Lydian capital of Sardis, Croesus refuses to yield to slavery. Instead, he 'caused a pyre to be built in front of his bronze-walled courtyard' (line 31) and there 'he bade an attendant kindle the wooden pile' (lines 48–9), on which he had already set his wife and daughters. On Myson's amphora, however, it is the king alone who piously pours his last libation while his attendant kindles the wood. Just as Myson has not included any attempt at rescue by Antiope's sister-Amazons – though they turn out in force on his Naples *psykter*[22] – so Croesus' family is absent from the scene as extraneous participants. If these references to a recent Lydian monarch, however philhellenic, are somewhat unexpected in their epinician contexts, the choice of this subject as the decoration of an Attic vase is, as Boardman says, 'unique' and likely somehow to be related to the scene of Theseus' Rape.[23]

Part of the strangeness of this programme lies in its combination of a mythical subject with an historical event of relatively recent memory, but I agree with John Boardman that, from an ideological standpoint, the two scenes may indeed be closely related. And I suggest that we can usefully turn to Herodotus for enlightenment. At Eretria we saw the same mythical subject, Theseus' Rape of Antiope, as a paradigm of the joint action taken by Eretria and Athens against Darius' western satrapy capital of Sardis. This campaign which culminated in their act of setting the city on fire is described by Herodotus as the 'beginning of evils for Greeks and barbarians', but, as Mary White has well argued, it was Cyrus' defeat of Croesus which Herodotus identified as his own starting-point for the history of the Persian Wars.[24] I therefore think it likely that Herodotus may be following an aetiology of the conflict developed earlier in the century and one which Myson's amphora itself strikingly reflects, its imagery reduced to essentials. Croesus' death was matched by the Athenian sack of Sardis which led, in its inexorable turn, to Persia's retaliation against Athens, and from the ashes of Xerxes' sack, Theseus' city rose triumphant, rescued, like Croesus, by the will of Zeus and dutiful to Apollo. This may be in part the point of the message which Bacchylides, so recently Athens' laureate, is presenting with allusive tact to his Dorian patron, and, were not my archaeological colleagues so adamant in their view that Myson had made his amphora some thirty years earlier, I would be inclined to think of it as a reflection of ideas first voiced in extant literature by the Cean nightingale – and I would think of what Professor Boardman has called a 'busy rape' on a cup in Oxford (Fig. 29)[25] as an image of the rape of Sardis with the Amazon cavalry pursuing Theseus' countrymen across the sea until their campaign was repulsed at Marathon. Whether the symposiast might find in Theseus' success with Antiope any precedent for some similar action towards his local barmaid, the painter of the Oxford cup (Fig. 30)[26] does not record. At any rate, for those of us who, despite Jacoby, follow Wilamowitz in treating a sixth-century *Theseid* as if it were non-existent (see p. 44) there is no hindrance, from that standpoint at least, to our considering the possibility that Oltos' design was conceived in a post-Marathonian context.

Simonides died in the year in which his nephew, Bacchylides, honoured Hiero's victory at Olympia, and it will be evident to most of you that the epigraph for this chapter on 'silent poetry' is taken from that oft-quoted dictum attributed to Simonides, that 'painting is silent poetry, and poetry speaking painting'.[27] Considering the decorative programme of the Theseum as I discussed it in Chapter 3, I hope you will share my judgement that W.B. Stanford was being unusually perverse when he described this observation as 'one of the oldest fallacies in the European tradition'.[28] I shall here attempt to justify my sense of the appropriateness of Simonides' comparison, referring once again to Richard Hughes' recognition of the spoken word and visual image as complimentary vehicles of public information in societies where literacy is restricted. Works of art like the murals of the Theseum might well acquire for their audience in Cimonian Athens 'the force of history and the augury of revelation. Such public art made legends tangible and credible, inserting them unconditionally into the lives of their audience, compelling belief and so altering behaviour.'[29] The same is true of the monuments I shall mention in this chapter, all but one of which certainly date from the years shortly after Simonides' death. We begin outside the city at Marathon, move on across the mountains to the Boeotian town of Plataea, then to the great cult centres of Olympia and Delphi which Bacchylides has instructed us to honour, and finally return to the centre of Athens.

As the Athenians encamped around the Shrine of Heracles on the plain of Marathon discussing their strategy, reinforcements arrived from their allies at Plataea, and together with Athenian and Plataean troops fought their way to victory in the subsequent battle. And eleven years later, on the battlefield of Plataea, Athens again took the field with her Boeotian allies who were led, as they had been at Marathon, by Arimnestus. Pausanias describes several Plataean monuments which record this campaign,[30] including a marble altar and statue of Zeus the Deliverer, erected near the common Greek grave. Even in Pausanias' day, the Plataeans continued to hold a contest every five years known as the Eleutheria, Freedom Games 'in which the biggest prizes are for running; they run under arms in front of Zeus' altar – and the trophy dedicated by Greece for the battle of Plataea stands two miles further from the city'.[31] Plutarch describes at some length the ceremonies attendant on the Greek victory at Plataea in his *Life of Areistides*, the Athenian field-commander among them: an annual procession, beginning at daybreak and led by a trumpeter sounding the onset of battle. Then follow chariots laden with myrrh and garlands, and after them a black bull which they proceed to sacrifice while making supplication to Zeus and Hermes. Then in ceremonies reminiscent of Odysseus in the Underworld the Plataeans invite 'those valiant men who perished in the defence of Greece to join in the banquet and drink the libations of blood'.[32] Like the Eretrians at Olympia, the Plataeans dedicated a bronze bull to Delphic Apollo 'because', so Pausanias suggests, 'in throwing out the barbarous enemy, they won prosperity by violence, and that included ploughing a free soil'.[33]

But the chief Plataean war memorial I wish to discuss here is the sanctuary of Athena the Warrior, built, Pausanias tells us,

> from booty of the battle of Marathon, which Athens awarded them. The statue is gilded wood, but the face and hands and feet are Pentelic stone. The size is not far short of the bronze on the Acropolis which the Athenians themselves dedicated as a tithe from the contest at Marathon, and it was Pheidias who made the statue of Athena for Plataea as well as in Athens. There are pictures in the temple, one by Polygnotus of Odysseus slaying the suitors and another by Onasias of the first Argive expedition against Thebes. These pictures are on the walls of the front chamber; at the feet of the great cult statue is a portrait-statue of Arimnestus.[34]

According to Plutarch, however, this temple of Athena Areia with its cult image was financed by the eighty talents which the Greek victors, accepting Areistides' counsel, had set apart for the Plataeans as their share in the spoils from the battle fought upon their territory, and most scholars nowadays favour Plutarch's account. On the other hand, the presence of Arimnestus, the Plataean commander at Marathon (and, as we shall see, perhaps the iconography itself), may define the sanctuary as a memorial of both campaigns. I shall return to this point in my next chapter, but for the moment I am concerned with the paintings which, even in Plutarch's day, still 'retained their lustre'.[35]

In view of their close military alliance, it is unsurprising that the Plataeans chose Athena Areia as the deity they honoured, for reasons comparable with those which led to her dominating presence on the west gable of Apollo's temple at Eretria. One wonders whether Polygnotus' commission to depict the 'Ate of the Suitors' was in any way influenced by his Athenian patron, Cimon.[36] Indeed, it is not unlikely that Cimon would have been glad to support the decoration of a memorial designed at least in part to honour Plataean loyalty at Marathon. At any rate, in terms of their architectural disposition in the porch of the sanctuary, the two paintings formed a matching pair, though apparently they were executed by different artists. Is there any corresponding relationship between their subjects, the *Septem* and *Suitors Slain?*

In general terms, their programme can be simply summarized: the *Septem* depicts the moment prior to battle when peaceful settlement has been refused, the *Suitors Slain*, the moment immediately after when the settlement has been enforced. Not only do we see a contrast between the aggressive Seven and the defeated Suitors, but also a clear reference to recent historical events. In the *Septem* the polis resists the enforced return of tyranny from outside; in the Odyssean scene the legitimate ruler has returned as an outsider to expel, and indeed, destroy the suitors who have invaded his house. These paintings thus provide in mythical terms a brilliant evocation of recent experience at Marathon and Plataea, as Friedrich Gottlieb Welcker already perceived in 1836.[37] I spoke of Cimon, but where is Theseus? *Ouk aneu Theseos*, 'not without Theseus', became a watchword of the Athenian fifth century,[38] but Plataea apparently did not choose to include any reference to Athena's new champion in this new temple of their protective divinity. Not explicitly perhaps, but the presence of Theseus may lurk beneath the surface of both these scenes.

The Polygnotan *Suitors Slain* plainly recalls the dénouement of the Odyssean Contest of the Bow when, against all apparent odds, the disguised beggar, under the continuing patronage of Athena, supplicates Apollo to guide his bow against the strangers, albeit (like the Medes and Persians) ancient kin who have invaded his house and sought to dispossess him of all ancestral property. At the centre of the suitors' contest in Odyssey 21, we pause to hear Antinous tell Odysseus the parable of the Lapith Wedding, so rudely disrupted by the centaur Eurytion. In 480 Athens with Poseidon's help had routed the fleet at Salamis, and in the next year had finally driven the invader from her sacred soil, not, however, before marauding centaurs had desecrated Demeter's temple at Eleusis and destroyed the olive groves which formed so traditional a staple of Athenian economy. We might well compare the outside of the cup in Munich (Fig. 31),[39] whose tondo (Fig. 20) Susan Woodford attempted to identify as the central image of the Centauromachy in Theseus' shrine but the mural may

75

also have reflected the Homeric tale which attributes future centauromachies to Eurytion's misconduct at Peirithous' Thessalian wedding feast. The better to understand the relationship between such centauromachies and the theme of *Suitors Slain*, I suggest an Homeric interlude which will in due course lead us to Olympia, and thence back to Plataea.

'Most things in Greece', Pausanias remarks, 'are subject to dispute' [40] and in the century following the excavations of the architectural sculpture from the Temple of Zeus at Olympia, almost every aspect of its evidence has aroused controversy. How, for example, do we judge the relationships among the major pedimental figures and, in some cases, even their individual identity? What was the original arrangement of the twelve metopes, depicting Heracles' Labours? Who were the sculptors and what artistic traditions did they represent? Finally, does the exterior decoration of the Temple reflect a unified compositional programme with an evident manifesto, a comprehensive ideology, or should we rest content, for example, with the view that the scenes retain 'something of the separateness of archaic architectural sculpture', that they were not organized 'according to a plan for the exposition of a theme or concept, . . . [but] simply for their pan-hellenic geographical associations'?[41]

Pausanias' own account of the monument has in different measure fuelled every one of these uncertainties. On the other hand, when he acknowledged that an honest attempt to ascertain accurate information about the past can often be thwarted by divergent traditions, Pausanias was not referring to Olympia, but to conflicting claims advanced by Thessaly, Euboea and Messenia as to the authentic site of Eurytus' far-famed citadel of Oechalia. Though he was intrigued by Thessaly's argument that the abandoned region of Eurytion was formerly known as Oechalia, our traveller decided in favour of the Messenian town for the somewhat credulous reason that Eurytus' bones were supposedly buried there. Eurytus, Eurytion, Thessaly: all belong to the story I want to tell, but Pausanias has, with some justice, been called the 'Prince of Digressors,'[42] and if I am to guide you expeditiously to our Athenian destination in 'The Future that Was', I cannot any longer afford the discursive leisure of Pausanias' genial companionship, but like Pindar and his Apollonian herald must aim direct, if from a distance, at my goal.

In his influential 'Reflections on *Ate* and *Hamartia*',[43]

R.D. Dawe criticized the view that, in Homer, *ate* and its cognate verb *aasamen* denote what we might speak of as 'delusion, mental blindness, *Verblendung*'. Dawe sought support for his judgement in what he calls the 'particularly striking . . . fact that it [scil., *ate*] is never used to refer to the conduct of the suitors in the Odyssey'.[44] In a strictly literal sense Dawe's observation is correct. Nonetheless, the suitors' conduct, as I have argued elsewhere,[45] is unmistakably (if indirectly) characterized in just those terms. I therefore wish to summarize here the ways in which such a conclusion can contribute to our understanding of the iconographic programme of the pedimental sculptures at Olympia and the ethical manifesto which they signify. Many roads lead to Olympia and I have chosen to set out from Oechalia and her Homeric court of Eurytus, for Eurytus through his arrogant folly challenged Apollo to a contest of the bow. When Apollo in wrath (*kholosamenos*)[46] responded by killing him, Eurytus' bow became the possession of Iphitus, his son, and this was the bow Odysseus accepted as a guest-gift in significant exchange for those more typically heroic weapons of sword and spear. This then was the bow which Penelope, at the opening of Odyssey 21, takes from the inner chamber to provide the suitors with a trial of strength and skill, a contest in which she herself was to be the prize, the contest which Antinous mindlessly proclaims will be a contest without *ate* for the suitors (*mnesteressin aethlon aaaton*).[47] Antinous now feigns ingenuousness, 'for I do not suppose this smoothly polished bow will easily be strung as none among us here is Odysseus' match: I myself have seen him – how well my memory remains – though I was still a child scarce able to speak'. Antinous' words conceal his true aspiration 'to string the bowcord and shoot the arrow through the iron'. Yet as Homer at once assures us, it was to be Antinous' destiny 'first to taste the arrow from Odysseus' blameless hands', and so it was.

Antinous, as his very name suggests, has again failed to connect evidence with mind. He has seen Odysseus (*ego de min autos opopa*), his recollection is clear (*kai gar mnemon eimi*),[48] but he still cannot recognize the man whom he now dishonours in his own house (*hon tot' atima / hemenos en megarois*).[49] He thinks to fool his companions, but he fools himself as well. So, in Book 2, when Penelope was caught thread-handed, unravelling her web,[50] Antinous thinks he has her outwitted, not recognizing that the shroud she weaves for Laertes[51] she weaves for them and that by coercing her to complete it she only forwards their own doom, a point Amphimedon ruefully records for Agamemnon when the suitors foregather in Hades, remembering Antinous' own words. 'Wait before hastening my marriage', Penelope had requested, 'wait until I finish the shroud' (*eis ho ke pharos / ekteleso*).[52] At last the time has come, the terms of marriage set, and the contest of the bow ordained, but the suitors have failed in their attempt to string Odysseus' bow and to win his wife. Then Odysseus throws off all beggarly disguise and hurls Antinous' rash words back in his teeth: *houtos men de aethlos aaatos ektetelestai*, 'this contest without *ate* is now indeed at its end'.[53]

Odysseus repudiates Antinous' failure not so much to string the bow, but to perceive how his proposition of the contest – and indeed the suitors' presence and their conduct in his house – was, from the start, instinct with *ate*. Not only have the suitors 'deluded' themselves, but Antinous' recent conceit of a 'contest without *ate*' has brought them to the brink of catastrophe as Odysseus now wields Eurytus' bow and aims his shaft straight at the throat of Antinous whence blood and not the wine he had been about to drink gushes forth. The suitors angrily rebuke Odysseus for his *kaka erga* – they themselves have yet to recognize him (*xeine, kakos andron toxazeai*)[54] – but Odysseus, unlike Eurytus, has committed no sacrilege since as soon as he called their contest to its close, he piously invoked the aid of Apollo in thus healing his house from the plague which had obsessed it these many years:

> *nun aute skopon allon, hon ou po tis balen aner,*
> *eisomai, ai ke tuchomi, porei de moi eukos Apollon.*

'Now watch me hit a mark no man has hit before: so grant my prayer, Apollo.'[55]

On Scheria, the young Phaeacian suitors for the hand of their princess Nausicaa taunt the stranger for his age and goad him to compete in their *pentathlon*.[56] Odysseus finally accepts their challenge and proceeds to hurl a huge discus far beyond their range. In a gesture of self-revelation they fail to perceive, Odysseus then proclaims his prowess as an archer at Troy, ceding first place only to Philoctetes,[57] but there is to be no archery contest on Scheria: Apollo's instrument of war is transferred to one of peace as Odysseus instead shoots from his mind in song. As Apollo *hekebolos* 'shoots from afar', so Telemachus, by his name and nature, 'fights at a distance'. Like his father, however, Telemachus enjoys

Apollo's protection for he returns to Ithaca in the company of the seer Theoclymenus, Mantius' grandson and the cousin of Argive Amphiaraus.[58] Theoclymenus promptly affirms his richly Apollonian heritage by a demonstration of augury. Just as Telemachus has finished telling Theoclymenus of the suitors' siege upon his father's household, 'a bird swooped to the right of him, a hawk, swift messenger of Apollo, tearing at the dove in its claws'.[59] For Theoclymenus, the hawk's omen is clear and he turns to Telemachus with these words:

Telemakh' ou toi aneu theou eptato dexios ornis,

'a god spoke in this bird on the right. . . . No house in Ithaca is kinglier than yours and your family's power shall prevail for ever'.[60] At *Odyssey* 20.243, while the suitors again plot Telemachus' death, 'a trembling dove is held in the talons of an eagle soaring above them', for Zeus is about to thunder his assent to their destruction.[61] The hawk, however, is particularly Apollo's predator and the dove its natural prey.[62] You will remember how Achilles tied the dove for a target in the archery contest which brought the Funeral Games of Patroclus near to their close.[63] Once the Odyssean contest is nearing its own end and the suitors have all been massacred, the disloyal maidservants who 'have loaded insults upon my own head and my mother's, and have slept with the suitors', these women 'are strung up by Telemachus like doves trapped in the thicket to which they have come back to nest'. They struggle with their feet for a little, but not for long,[64] and then Melanthius, son of Dolius, is brought out to the forecourt and the men 'cut off his nose, his ears, his hands, and his feet, and throw his genitals for dogs to eat'.[65]

Melanthius, black traitor to Odysseus' house, had had charge of the goats and the wine. The implications of this combination are made clear in Book 9 when, in his first encounter after leaving Troy, Odysseus raids the Cicones, erstwhile Trojan allies and themselves devotees of Apollo. Apollo's priest, Euanthes' son, gives Odysseus a goatskin of wine. Apollo's presence is next implicit on Goat Island.[66] The men of Odysseus' twelve ships go forth to shoot the native game and their catch is divided nine to each boat and ten for Odysseus:[67] 108 plus 10, exactly the complement of suitors and their ten servants whom Odysseus will execute at his homecoming,[68] a slaughter likewise conducted under Apollo's patronage. When sun sets on Goat Island, Odysseus

79

and his men feast upon their goats and drink Ciconian wine, but across the bay on the following day, how comparable and yet how utterly changed is the hideous feast of the goatherd, Polyphemus. In the *Odyssey*, Odysseus himself exemplifies Apollonian injunctions against excess and on behalf of self-knowledge. On the other hand, drunkenness is disorderly and Athena's olive, in collaboration with Apollo's wine, wreak Odysseus' revenge upon the ogre 'who has no regard for aegis-bearing Zeus'[69] or the social contract of his code of hospitality. The fate of the goatherd Melanthius, though more elaborately brutal, is also reminiscent of another's we have yet to meet. Earlier in the day, all the suitors including Eurymachus, but with the exception of Antinous, had tried to string Odysseus' bow and have failed. Now Antinous alone awaits his turn, but proposes to postpone the decision (*all' hekeloi / katthete*):[70] 'break out good wine and fill our cups. At tomorrow's dawn bid Melanthius the goatherd bring his prize goats so that we may offer thighbones to Apollo, famous for archery, then try the bow and end the contest' (*ekteleomen aethlon*),[71] but for the suitors there will be no dawn, only the one long night which Theoclymenus has foretold. Since the contest was announced, Odysseus has not addressed the suitors, but now he does so: 'how nicely Antinous just spoke, counselling you to stop the trial and turn your thoughts to gods. Tomorrow god shall grant power to whom he wills. But come, give me the smooth bow that I may try my hand and strength at it.'[72]

On Scheria, Odysseus had explicitly refrained from any comparison between his own skill as a bowman and that of Heracles or 'Oechalian Eurytus, . . . for Apollo took his challenge ill, and killed him'.[73] This reticence is doubtless associated with the fact that Odysseus did not take the bow of Eurytus to Apollo's Troy, but left it at home secure in storage. Just as no archery contest was tried on Scheria, but instead reserved for Ithaca, so Eurytus' bow has been saved to become again an instrument of Apollonian trial. Like Eurytus, the suitors have no power against Apollo (who, as at Troy, fights to defend a household and a kingdom under siege), for the suitors are Apollo's ethical foe, both in their excess and in their failure – epitomized in the name of Antinous – to know themselves. As a consequence they both lack the capacity to be successful archers and naturally become a target for Apollo's protégés.

In a memorable passage at the end of Book 20, Athena 'drove

the suitors' reasoning to wander off-course' (*pareplanxen de noema*),[74] in pointed contrast to the nature of Odysseus' own wandering. Amid the suitors' raucous laughter Theoclymenus foresees the doom of these 'lost, sad men already shrouded in night . . . as the fair walls and pedestals around us drip crimson blood and the courtyard fills with shades bound for Erebus'.[75] Athena and Apollo again collaborate to restore Odysseus to his home and reorder unrule. It is time, Athena decides, to 'try those dogs at archery, to usher bloody slaughter in'[76] and Penelope goes off to fetch the bow for 'the contest without *ate*'.

While the *ate* of the suitors is an inevitable consequence of Athena's act of thus 'driving their reason off-course', they were afflicted with *ate* from the moment they began to infest Odysseus' house with their drunken revel. Nowhere is this condition more clearly illuminated than in Antinous' reply to Odysseus' request to try the bow and thereby participate implicitly in the competition for Penelope's hand. Antinous recalls the cautionary tale of the Lapith Wedding and its disruption by an unruly guest. The Lapiths, descended from Apollo, have gathered to celebrate the marriage of Peirithous, their king. The centaur, Eurytion, the offspring of rape – and surely the eponymous ancestor of Pausanias' Thessalian Oechalia – becomes drunk with wine and, thus maddened, runs amuck through Peirithous' house:

> *mainomenos kak'erexe domon kata Peirithooio.*[77]

Wine has filled his *phrenes* with *ate* and he acts accordingly, drunk and disorderly. Elpenor, Odysseus' *Doppelgänger*,[78] readily acknowledged in the Underworld that his own fatal downfall resulted from similar cause and effect[79] and now Antinous characterizes Eurytion's behaviour in order to suggest that the parable applies to Odysseus. On the contrary, this exemplum of the drunken centaur, with its cadenza upon the theme of *ate*,[80] offers an unmistakeable image of Antinous' own behaviour as a loutish guest at Odysseus' court. By his abusive conduct and, in particular, his desire to intrude upon the marriage of a household in which he is a drunken guest, Antinous' outrage replicates Eurytion's. Though Eurytion's punishment foreshadows that of Melanthius, the last of Odysseus' enemies to face execution, the conditions of Eurytion and Antinous, the first to die, are nonetheless closely comparable. It was wine that confounded Eurytion; and Eurytion, the source of strife between centaurs and

Lapiths,[81] first brought harm upon himself because he was 'heavy with wine' (*oinobareion*).[82] How appropriate then that Antinous is shot at the moment of raising the goblet to his lips and that his dying act, an involuntary reflex, is to kick over a table at the feast.[83] The Lapiths are sons of Apollo and so is Odysseus who now wields Eurytus' bow, no longer used in sacrilege, but to wreak just vengeance, divinely sanctioned. The centaurs prefigure the suitors and the actions of the suitors and centaurs alike thus exemplify the domain of *ate*.

I therefore suggest that, to an Homeric audience of fifth-century Greeks, the Centauromachy at the feast could be perceived as an image of *ate* and that Lapith survival depended in part upon the controlling presence of their divine ancestor Apollo, seen in Odyssean terms. Apollo commands the action on the west pediment at Olympia not merely because, as Bernard Ashmole has eloquently remarked, he is 'son of Zeus, patron of all the arts, and of all that makes life humane and decent',[84] but because the parable of the Lapith Wedding from Homer's Odyssey underlies his presence there. Martin Robertson has made the interesting observation that the women set into the far angles of the pediment are 'sleepers in another part of the house, roused and frightened by clamour in the hall, something like Penelope and her women listening to the fight with the suitors'.[85]

Many influences undoubtedly converged to identify this image of the Lapith Feast as the subject most appropriate to decorate the west pediment at Olympia, but this is not the place to dwell in detail on my view of the compositional programme of the temple as a whole, the Heraclean metopes, the relation between the two marriages on either gable, or the mythological allusion to the main events of chariot-race and pancration they respectively make. I can only mention their ethical message. I might mention in passing that in my view recent attempts to interpret the manifesto of the east pediment in the light of Pindar's first *Olympian* are beside the mark,[86] for Pindar's recasting of a traditional tale is chiefly motivated by the immediate circumstances of his patronage. Regardless of Pindar's privately held views about divine conduct, we must remember that Hiero took special pride in his role as high priest of the Syracusan cult of Demeter and Kore, so that any talk of Demeter as *gastrimargos* would likely be construed as a tactless affront to his patron. It is therefore the particular circumstances of the composition of this ode, not radical developments in any more widely held Greek view of the myth which have motivated Pindar's innovation, and I am therefore content to see in the east gable at Olympia a warning against *dolos*, a warning which Zeus *dikaios* oversees and a warning which all competitors who have taken their oaths at the altar of Zeus *horkios* have themselves consciously accepted.

While it may be customary enough for an east gable to include some apotropaic statement and the west a fight, at Olympia tradition and contemporary ethics fuse, for warning against *dolos* and the inevitable consequences of *ate* are inextricably linked in the statements of contemporary poets: Aeschylus' *Persians*, Pindar's second and third *Pythians* provide obvious contexts among many, and it is surely significant for our argument that the collocation in the second *Pythian*[87] occurs as a crucial part of Pindar's aetiology of the generation of centaurs.

'When we came to the real Olympia', J.H. Mahaffy wrote in the 1870s,

the prospect was truly disenchanting. However interesting excavations may be, they are always exceedingly ugly. Instead of grass and flowers, and pure water, we found the classic spot defaced with great mounds of earth, and trodden bare of grass. We found the Kladeus flowing a turbid drain into the larger river. We found hundreds of workmen, and wheelbarrows, and planks, and trenches, instead of solitude and the song of birds. Thus it was that we found the famous temple of Zeus.[88]

Let us exchange this 'disenchanting prospect' of Olympia, ruined by earthquake and rendered unsightly by excavation, and return to Plataea where the Centauromachy at the Feast, with Theseus and Peirithous as joint protagonists – the scene which I think most probably formed the subject of the mural in Theseus' shrine – has now been referred to its Homeric source, as the action of the *Odyssey*, no longer only its myth, prefigures the role of Theseus as he arrives at his ancestral home. And, like Odysseus, he does so after overcoming many obstacles along the way and enters his house, as Bacchylides reminds us, at first unrecognized. With no less determination than Odysseus, however, Theseus also comes to drive the strangers from the gate. The scene of *Suitors Slain* not only became a subject for Athenian vase-painting, but also formed part of the decoration of the hero's shrine at Gjölbaschi-Trysa in

Lycia, which included throughout its remarkable programme so many reminiscences of the art and iconography of Cimonian Athens.[89]

We do not really know when the sanctuary of Athena Areia at Plataea was dedicated, but a date during the second quarter of the fifth century seems probable. The Boeotian theme of the *Seven*, appropriate enough at Plataea, was chosen by Aeschylus as the subject of a play produced in 467 in which many scholars have noticed reflections of recent wars. Some might therefore prefer to see the Plataean paintings at roughly the same period as Aeschylus' *Septem* rather than place them in the later decade of the First Peloponnesian War. Nonetheless, Onasias' *Seven* could well memorialize the Argive-Athenian setback at Tanagra at the same time implying the Epigoni and the promise of Oenophyta to come, while *Suitors Slain* evokes in its Boeotian context the punishment due to Medes and Medisers alike. In this connection we may also recall the tradition that Theseus led his citizens out to war with Thebes so he might recover the bodies of the Argive dead and give them due burial.

Theseus' action apparently formed the subject of Aeschylus' *Eleusinioi*[90] as well as providing a basis for the Athenian claim, in Herodotus' report of their speech, that they deserved to fight on the right wing at the Battle of Plataea.[91] For these and other reasons – though 'the comment is subjective' – I tentatively prefer this late date for the paintings at least in terms of what I interpret as the likely intent of their iconography. Moreover, there is a rumour that Cimon, not yet recalled from ostracism, was nevertheless in evidence at the Battle of Tanagra. May we see the decoration of Athena's sanctuary at Plataea in this context? Athena the Warrior, not simply Polias, would be a thoroughly appropriate manifestation for a divinity patrolling the border of Attica. It is surely significant to note that the Ephebic Oath designates Athena by this very term,[92] and Bacchylides showed us, as we saw in Chapter 3, how important a role the ephebes played in Cimon's Thesean ideology.

I have spoken in this chapter of war memorials and in the next I shall discuss some aspects of the tradition by which those who had participated in victory and even glorious defeat were memorialized in verse. In response to the reality of mounting numbers of Athenian war-dead, casualties of campaigns in defence of the fatherland at home and in pursuit of empire abroad, Athens built

1   A pottery drinking vessel of a kind which may have been influenced by vessels of precious metal acquired as booty from the Persians.

2   The Great King Darius protected by a sunshade; a relief from the eastern door of the Main Hall of the Palace of Xerxes at Persepolis.

3 A marble statue of an Amazon from the Temple of Apollo Daphnephorus at Eretria, but found in Rome in the grounds of the Villa Ludovisi.

4   Athena, the central
figure of the west pediment
of the Temple of Apollo
Daphnephorus at Eretria.

5   Theseus and Antiope,
the Amazon queen, from
the pedimental sculpture of
the Temple of Apollo
Daphnephorus at Eretria.

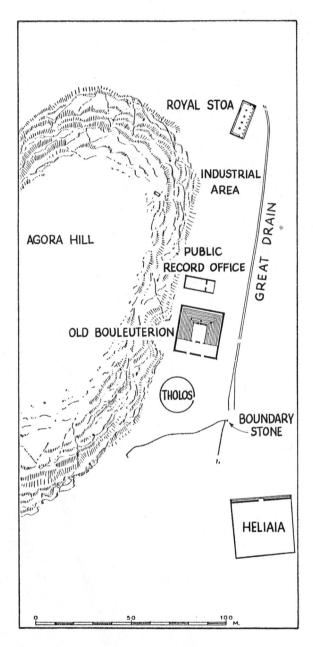

6 The Tholos (the residence of the council presidents), the Old Bouleuterion (the Council Chamber), the Public Record Office, and the Royal Stoa were the first public buildings erected by the Ephialtic/Periclean democracy in the 450s BC.

7   The Temple of Aphaia at Aegina.

8   The Court of Darius, the Great King of Persia, shown on the eve of the departure of the Persian army for Greece in 490. This scene appears on the Darius crater, made in Southern Italy in the fourth century BC.

9   Bellerophon and the Chimaera, on the reverse of the Darius crater.

10 Greeks slaying Amazons, on the front neck of the Darius crater.

11 A Greek hoplite shown in the moment of victory over a fallen Persian warrior.

a   *b*

12   Another, more metaphorical, rendering of Greek victory over Persia. The oriental states 'I am Eurymedon, I stand bent over'.

13   The Sack of Troy from the shoulder of a pottery water jar. Priam is attacked by Neoptolemus at an altar of Apollo, while behind him Ajax rapes Cassandra at a shrine of Athena.

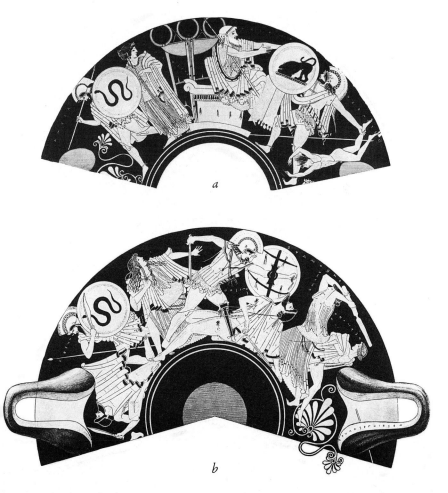

14 The Sack of Troy on an Attic cup. Neoptolemus attacks Priam with
the body of his grandson Astyanax. Elsewhere Andromache wields a pestle
against a Greek soldier.

15 The Battle between Gods and Giants: Poseidon and Hephaestus
fight back to back against a common foe.

16 On the back of the cup in Figure 15, Athena leads Zeus to the
battlefield from his Olympian palace.

17   In the tondo of the cup in Figures 15 and 16 is an image of Selene – perhaps a representation of a lunar eclipse.

18   Poseidon's victory is given the greater prominence on this cup; not only is he shown in the centre of the front, but in the interior as well.

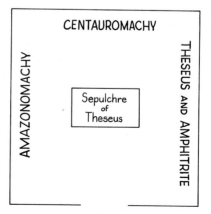

19   A hypothetical plan of the (lost) Theseum at Athens.

20   A Greek hoplite soldier kills a centaur: an image which may be
associated with the Centauromachy in Cimon's Theseum.

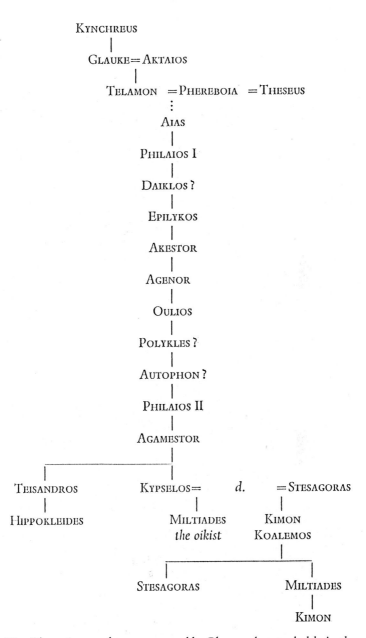

KYNCHREUS
|
GLAUKE = AKTAIOS
|
TELAMON = PHEREBOIA = THESEUS
⋮
AIAS
|
PHILAIOS I
|
DAIKLOS ?
|
EPILYKOS
|
AKESTOR
|
AGENOR
|
OULIOS
|
POLYKLES ?
|
AUTOPHON ?
|
PHILAIOS II
|
AGAMESTOR
|

TEISANDROS   KYPSELOS =   d.   = STESAGORAS
| | |
HIPPOKLEIDES   MILTIADES   KIMON
                     the oikist   KOALEMOS
                                                          |

                    STESAGORAS   MILTIADES
                                                          |
                                                        KIMON

21 Cimon's genealogy composed by Pherecydes, probably in the 470s BC.

22 Theseus stands before Athena in her temple on the front of a pottery cup made at Athens.

23 Theseus in the court of his divine father, Poseidon, and Amphitrite, his stepmother; the back of the cup in Figure 22.

24 In the interior of the cup in Figures 22 and 23, Theseus is greeted by
Amphitrite, his marine stepmother, who presents him with tokens of
sovereignty and prestige.

25 Theseus is supported by his divine half-brother, Triton, in the presence of Athena and Amphitrite.

26 The drunken party-goers on this pottery wine-mixing bowl have been interpreted as a parody of the Tyrannicides.

27 Croesus on the pyre at the fall of Sardis.

28 Theseus' Rape of Antiope, on the back of the pottery amphora in Figure 27.

29 The Rape of Antiope on an Athenian pottery cup.

30 The interior of the cup in Figure 29: a slave-girl is perhaps a secular analogue for Theseus' capture of Antiope.

31 Greek soldiers battle with Centaurs who are armed with stylized olive trees.

W

I OENOE		II AMAZONOMACHY	III TROY TAKEN	IV BATTLE OF MARATHON	
Mountains and Oenoe					
	arche			*akme* and *tolmemata*	Persian defeat
Shrine of Heracles	Plain of Marathon		ACRO|POLEIS of ATHENS|ILIUM		Persians in marsh	and ships
History		Myth		History	

E

32 The arrangement of the paintings in the Stoa Poikile in the Athenian Agora.

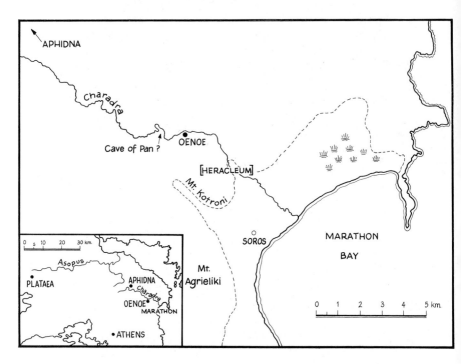

33 Marathon and its environs.

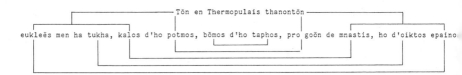

34 The structure of Simonides' lyric poem for the dead at Thermopylae.

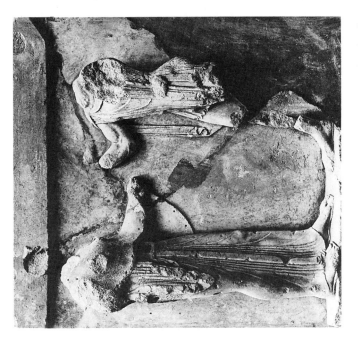

36 Athena and Theseus; a metope from the south side of the Athenian Treasury at Delphi.

35 Heracles and the Ceryneian hind; a metope from the north side of the Athenian Treasury at Delphi.

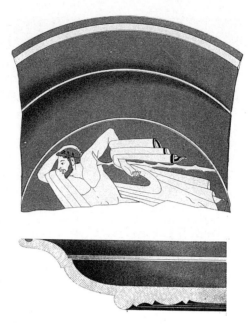

37 A fragmentary red-figured pottery plate found by Ludwig Ross on the Athenian Acropolis in the early 1830s, and which became the keystone of the chronology of Greek art proposed by Franz Studniczka in 1887, and adopted by Ernst Langlotz in 1920.

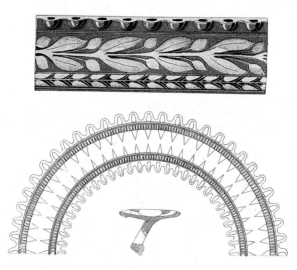

38 An elaborate pottery lamp, thought by Ross to antedate the Persian sack of Athens in 480/79 BC.

39 A pottery 'owl skyphos' considered by Ross to have suffered in the Persian sack of Athens.

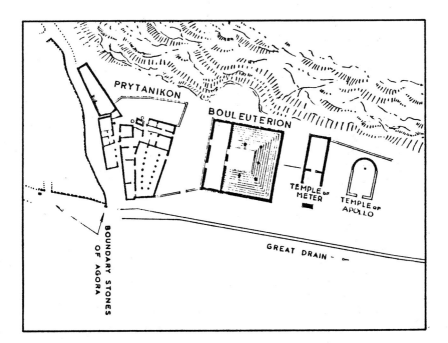

40 A plan of the west side of the Athenian Agora made in 1970, in which the building immediately to the north of the Old Bouleuterion is identified as the 'Temple of Meter'.

a public cemetery – again, some have supposed that this was Cimon's doing – and introduced the ceremony of the *logos epitaphios*, the Funeral Speech which celebrated the heroism of those who had died by placing their sacrifice in the glorious traditions of their mythical ancestors. Thus the memory of their renown might be imperishable, *kleos aphthiton* indeed. Pindar brilliantly invokes this cast of immortality when he sings of Xenocrates' Pythian victory on the eve of Marathon: For Xenocrates is built

> a treasure-house of song, ready within the valley of Apollo,
> rich in golden gifts. And that treasure neither wind nor
> wintry rain-storms coming from strange lands, as a fierce host
> born of thunderous cloud, shall drive into the hiding places
> of the sea, to be beaten by the all-sweeping drift.[93]

C.M.Bowra is surely mistaken in his confidence that Pindar's ode 'gives no hint that he foresaw what was coming or was even aware that the Persians were on the move'.[94] The imagery of these lines and the pointed use of words like *epaktos* and *stratos* clearly imply the advance of a hostile army even against the protected glens of Apollonian Delphi: so place your aspiration, Xenocrates of Acragas, not in material wealth, but in the incorruptibility of my song. Yet it is of 'silent poetry', not 'speaking painting' that I should talk and it is time to go to Marathon, not to the battlefield itself, but across from Theseus' shrine to the northwest corner of the Athenian Agora, to a building which faced directly on to Athens' city centre.

'Imagine yourselves at the Stoa Poikile', Aeschines declared, 'for the monuments of all your glories are in the Agora'.[95] The Tyrannicide monument stood nearby and in the Stoa itself the bronze shields of the Skionians and their allies were still displayed in Pausanias' day, together with spoils taken from the Spartans at Sphacteria.[96] Among the paintings of the Stoa, the *Battle of Marathon* was especially famous. Not only was it a great monument of past glory, but 'probably the most celebrated picture in the city'.[97] Unless Himerius' testimony was merely a rhetorical conceit affected in the aftermath of the Herulian sack,[98] the Marathon remained extant in the middle of the fourth century AD. On the other hand, by the time Synesius of Cyrene visited Athens in 402, all the paintings had been removed from the Stoa and the city at large now reminded its visitor of 'the bare hide of a sacrificial victim, . . . a token of what the living animal had once been'.[99]

According to Pausanias the *Battle of Marathon* was the 'last' (*teleutaion*)[100] in a series of four murals. Besides the *Marathon*, Pausanias describes 'in the middle of the walls'[101] a battle of Athenians fighting with Theseus against Amazons and, 'next to this Amazonomachy' (*epi de tais Amazosin*), Polygnotus' scene of *Troy Taken* which included a joint council called by the Greek leaders to discuss Locrian Ajax's rape of Cassandra. The first scene, so Pausanias tells us (*haute de he stoa prota men* . . .),[102] depicted 'Athenian forces marshalled in Argive Oenoe against Spartans'. The conflict, however, has not yet reached its crisis. On the contrary, the battle is only just beginning and the combatants are said still to be in the process of engaging: *alla arkhomene te he makhe kai es kheiras eti suniontes.*[103]

Subjects like the *Battle of Marathon*, an *Amazonomachy* or a *Troy Taken* belong to the world of familiar Greek history and myth, but a *Battle of Argive Oenoe* — though 'still intermittently in the news'[104] — remains one of the most shadowy events (or non-events) of the Pentecontaetia. In the past some have sought its explanation in myth,[105] but today most scholars agree that such a battle (if it ever occurred) must have been a contemporary one. Moreover, 'the disposition of the paintings in the Stoa is', as Wycherley observes, 'purely conjectural'.[106] The building which was probably erected *c.* 460 seems to have been associated with Cimon, in that Cimon's brother-in-law, Peisianax, was 'in some sense responsible for its erection and provided the building with its first name, Stoa Peisianakteios'.[107] The prominence of Theseus in the decoration of the Stoa is also congruent with Cimonian influence. At the same time, Cimon fostered the memory of the Battle of Marathon not only to restore the reputation of his father Miltiades, but also to diminish that of his own political rival, Themistocles, victor at Salamis. Finally, Cimon had the reputation of favouring détente with Sparta. All these factors must be taken into account when we consider the decoration of a public building with potentially Cimonian associations. For example, a battle waged by Athenians against Spartans is hardly the subject we would expect to find displayed in such a building. Some scholars have answered this objection by identifying the battle as one fought only after Cimon's dismissal from Ithome in that the representation of such a contest might be regarded as suitable to the mood of those Athenians who had recently voted for Cimon's ostracism. Even so, an immediately contemporary battle is in itself an unexpected subject for a public monument in fifth-century Athens[108] and the juxtaposition of anti-Cimonian with pro-Cimonian propaganda in a building likely to have been erected in his honour is not especially plausible.

In a series of articles, Michael Vickers and I have discussed the issues I have raised.[109] We have argued that a battle probably did take place at Argive Oenoe in the early days of the First Peloponnesian War, but that this encounter was not the subject of the first painting Pausanias saw when he entered the Stoa Poikile. There were many factors which probably contributed to his conclusion that the painting represented a battle in the Peloponnese which he had other cause to suppose had actually occurred. In Chapter 3, I emphasized one of Pausanias' reasons for explaining at some length the subject of *Theseus' Dive* on the third wall of the hero's shrine: the myth was unfamiliar *dia ton khronon*, 'on account of the lapse of time'. In the case of Oenoe, time had been a more effective cormorant and devoured all recollection of the role of Marathonian Oenoe on the eve of the great battle, for it was by way of Oenoe, a hamlet of the Tetrapolis, up in the mountains overlooking the plain, that Arimnestus would have led his Plataean division on their forced march to answer their allies' call for help. We may therefore expect that the place of Oenoe was painted on the panel. Pausanias elsewhere acknowledges his confusion in distinguishing a representation of allies joining ranks from one of enemies *es kheiras suniontes*, 'joining battle'. We suspect that he has mistaken the sight of Plataean reinforcements tumbling down the gully below Oenoe with his image of Pleistarchus, the young Spartan king, leading his commandos down towards Argos one night some thirty years later over terrain which in the conventions of Early Classical muralism might have been represented in similar terms. As the Plataeans reach the Shrine of Heracles where the Athenians are encamped, the generals remain in doubt how best they should proceed, but in the event it was Miltiades' strategy that swayed his colleagues and ultimately won the day (or so, at any rate, our reports of the battle declare).

Let us envisage the four paintings set side by side on the rear wall of the Stoa in the order I have sketched out for you (Fig. 32): the first painting (the Oenoe) marks the strategic preliminaries I have just described, the Marathon panel on the far right shows the battle at its height with the Persians sinking into the marsh as they flee in disarray to their ships while Theseus rises from the earth of Attica to collaborate with other gods and heroes as if at Troy, but now working in unison to aid the men of Athens in defence of their liberty. And there, in the centre of the panel, stands Callimachus, the courageous field-general, shot through with arrows (like that sanctified pin-cushion, St Sebastian, his iconographical *epigonus*) but though Callimachus is strapped to no post, he does not collapse in defeat.

What of the two central panels, the *Amazonomachy* and *Troy Taken*? E.B. Harrison has shown that the iconography of the Parthenos shield was informed by that of the *Amazonomachy* in the Stoa.[110] The primary subject of the Parthenos shield appropriately represents the Amazonian siege of the Athenian Acropolis since Athena, in her role as Polias (not yet Parthenos and Promachos), shielded her citizens at the time of the Persian sack.[111] Harrison's reconstruction of the shield, however, by no means rules out the possibility that the painting in the Stoa also depicted the Amazonomachy on the plain of Marathon, the mythical antetype of historical events which occurred ten years earlier in 490. Indeed, on the basis of the fragment of a terracotta shield,[112] Harrison has suggested that 'the Amazonian pelta beside the feet of the dead Greek . . . could be a shorthand for the prime Marathonian symbols, Soros and Trophy.'

The *Amazonomachy* and *Troy Taken* were probably executed as bipartite paintings. On the left of the *Amazonomachy* we therefore reconstruct a plain, the plain of Marathon, mediating the council at Oenoe in the first painting and the sack of Athens to the right of the second. In this first pair of historical and mythical paintings, the Athenians are on the defensive against the oriental invader; in the pair to the right, these roles are reversed. In *Troy Taken*, Athenians no longer protect themselves courageously against barbarian assault. They have sacked an eastern citadel and rest victorious on the plain nearby, once again in council. In the *Marathon*, upon another plain, they proceed to rout the Persians and drive them to the marshes and the sea: arrest and movement / arrest and movement, framed in a Marathonian landscape. The victorious Greeks gather in the booty of the *khrusophoroi Medoi*. Both at Marathon and Eurymedon Athens can truly be said to have devastated Persian might (*estoresan dunamin*),[113] as Marathon initiated the destruction which Eurymedon brought to full harvest.

We need not now rehearse the counterpoint between the Trojan and the Persian Wars which plays so essential a part in the cultural imagery of the fifth century.[114] *Troy Taken* nicely brings together the 'gold-bearing Medes' and the Trojans, their characteristic mythical antetypes. That Athens profited from the booty of the Persian Wars is beyond doubt. Anecdotes of Callias Laccoplutus on the battlefield of Marathon,[115] the dedications of Persian spoils on the Acropolis, and the 'pavilions full of all manner of rich booty' won at the Eurymedon[116] unambiguously demonstrate this fact. In the centre of the composition the two Acropoleis of Athens and Troy are set side by side. Within the *Amazonomachy* we move in corresponding historical time from Marathon to the sack of Athens. The temporal scheme of *Troy Taken* may have suggested a parallel sequence. The fall of Troy has been thought to prefigure Cimon's capture of Eion[117] which was followed later on by his great victory at the Eurymedon. What victory upon Attic soil had initiated through his father's brilliant strategy, Cimon at last brought to completion as he destroyed Persia's might.

These paintings are arranged according to the typical argument of an epinician ode in which the victor and the occasion of his victory frame the central passage which typically celebrates his ancestors' triumphs or contemplates the significance of the victory from the standpoint of myth as *paideia*. If this analogy is valid, then Marathon is the particular *nike* being celebrated and the content of the epigram which was probably visible within the Stoa[118] is therefore fully congruent with this interpretation. More recent victories, however, have been cast in the conceptual framework of myths while Marathon itself is already assuming a place in the genealogy of heroic legend. It is evident that Cimon or his partisans did not choose to celebrate these triumphs in exclusively historical terms. In 472 Pericles and Aeschylus had remembered the Persian defeat at Salamis (and Plataea) in the form of a tragedy. The Greek victory was already being contemplated on a scale that transcended the particular. The grand formality of the paintings in the Stoa celebrates that victory in 'silent poetry' and praises Miltiades as its architect and epinician *laudandus*.

At the close of the last chapter, I promised I would show you a 'tomb with a view', and that is surely what could be seen in the Stoa, for in their discontinuous, but formally appropriate, landscape, the paintings depict the panorama of the battlefield of Marathon as it still presents itself to a spectator standing on top of the Soros. The Stoa Poikile brought Marathon to Athens and set the memory of the battle and the triumphs that flowed from it before the gaze of all.

The Stoa was erected on the north edge of the Agora, facing on to its centre. T. Leslie Shear, Jr, attributes 'its peculiar orientation NE–SW' to 'the broad double channel of the Eridanos River which runs nearly parallel to the S[outh]'.[119] The effect of this orientation, whatever factors may have determined its cause, would have been to set the spectator facing the view from the same direction as if he were standing on the Soros itself with the hills above Oenoe in the northwest and the marshes to the east.[120] This is the view Byron beheld as he stood atop the Marathon mound, and surely from that vantage point he conceived his famous couplet:

> The mountains look on Marathon
> And Marathon looks on the sea.

As one of his biographers has written, 'this spectacle kindled Byron and fired him with an emotion that was not to die.'[121] Imagine then how men and the sons of men who had themselves fought at that great battle must have reacted to this memorial of their most illustrious moment, 'silent poetry' speaking to them in the heart of their city.

5

TROPHIES FOR THE GODS

Imagine yourselves standing atop the Marathon mound (Fig. 32; cf. Fig. 33) some time towards the middle of the fifth century, gazing towards the hillside over on the left down which, as night fell, a full division of Plataeans had rushed at full pelt. They did so in order to reinforce their Athenian allies, gathered around the Shrine of Heracles, preparing to defend themselves and all of Greece against the Persian horde whose fleet waited off-shore, their infantry already camped out on the plain of Marathon by the eastern shore over there on your right. The Athenian generals are debating their best strategy and you may have been able to make out Miltiades energetically urging his own view. But as you look towards the east, the sun has risen and the quiet scene of anticipation is suddenly transformed. Now you see the battle at its crisis. At first the fighting is equal, but now the Persian wings are crumbling and the Greeks have converged upon the centre, driving the enemy back to their ships. The majority does not reach this haven, for we see them in unfamiliar terrain, losing their footing in the deadly marshes fed by a spring named in honour of Macaria, Heracles' daughter. And those who have escaped the marsh are being cut down as they attempt to board their ships. Such then, in outline, is the scene as you remember it many years later from the belvedere of the tomb originally erected to honour the 192 Athenian dead, but which perhaps had been enlarged during the period of Cimon's political leadership as a more substantial monument to that great victory.

Though I have been speaking of the battle itself my description of its climax follows Pausanias' account of the painting he saw in the Stoa Poikile across the northwest corner of the Athenian Agora.

91

His language implies a narrative sequence from left to right, for on the left of the panel, the fighting is still equally balanced, while 'the painting ends' – this is Pausanias' word – 'with the Phoenician ships, and the Greeks slaughtering barbarians as they jump into them.'[1] This narrative sequence, I suggested, stretches across the whole composition of all four panels from left to right, placed as they apparently were, side by side along the back wall of the Stoa. The first painting, the one I called the *Oenoe*, probably represented the moment of decision in the Athenian camp on the eve of the battle as their reinforcements arrived from Plataea, though admittedly, this is not how Pausanias described its subject matter. Though Oenoe played no part in the actual battle, the hamlet was prominently situated up in the hills overlooking the plain and the Plataeans must surely have passed by it on their way to join their fellow Greeks. I assume that the name 'Oenoe' was painted on the panel both as a topographical signpost and by virtue of her membership in the Marathonian tetrapolis. I suspect that the name referred not directly to the place itself, but to its local mountain nymph, corresponding to 'the hero Marathon' – I am quoting Pausanias again – from whom the *'level* [my italics] ground got its name' and whom the artist has depicted, standing on his own ground, thereby defining it. The human actors are, however, unnamed and the likelihood that the first and last paintings were by different artists may have been reflected in somewhat different representations of the same characters, thereby reinforcing Pausanias' assumption – influenced by his view that a battle had taken place at Argive Oenoe – that the two scenes were unrelated.

I am not dismayed by the fact that Oenoe is nowhere explicitly mentioned in ancient accounts of the narrative of the victory at Marathon for, as I have said, it had no direct part to play in the battle itself. On the other hand, Michael Vickers and I have speculated that we do indeed have a description of the subject of this painting, in a somewhat unexpected but entirely appropriate source, namely, Herodotus' own account of the campaign. For Herodotus' narrative of the preliminaries to the battle and the battle itself is divided into two equal, but thematically disproportionate halves, and many of the obvious inadequacies in his account of events preceding the battle, to which A.W. Gomme has drawn attention,[2] can be readily understood if this painting constituted a major source for his reconstruction.[3]

Before we leave the Stoa, however, on this disconcerting note that Pausanias may be in error (though, to quote John Boardman, 'he often is')[4] let me draw attention to certain other points based on his description of the Marathon. Besides the local hero, Marathon himself, Pausanias mentions, among other supernatural participants, Heracles, Athena and Theseus, and elsewhere in his narrative of Attica he identifies Heracles' daughter, Macaria, as the indigenous spirit of the marsh.[5] Many other ancient sources also describe the painting in more or less detail,[6] but, for my purposes at this point, Pausanias' information will suffice. If our reading of the first panel is correct, then Heracles' presence is also implicit in the topography of both scenes as well as explicit in the battle itself. In this connection we may note that the people of Marathon claim to have been the first to acknowledge that hero's divinity, and Pindar mentions the games they held in his honour.[7] At the same time, however, Pausanias describes the figure of Theseus, rising from the very soil of Marathon as he comes to the aid of his people.[8]

To my mind, however, this image provides a striking declaration of Attic autochthony on the part of a hero otherwise known to be the son of Poseidon and born in Troezen. The tradition that Plutarch records to the effect that 'many soldiers believed they saw an apparition of Theseus in arms, rushing on in the lead against the barbarians' probably derives, if not from the picture itself, at least from the propaganda that inspired it.[9] Theseus is also prominent in Marathonian legend as the hero who finally subdued the Cretan bull which sired the Minotaur and which Heracles had brought to Eurystheus' court. But the point to which I wish to draw particular attention is that the worship of Heracles at Marathon prior to the battle is clearly established by the presence of his shrine (not to mention his daughter's spring) and that Theseus rises up out of the same Marathonian soil to join him in defeat of the barbarian foe.

I described the formality of the four paintings in the Stoa as that of an epinician ode (see p. 89). The analogy is appropriate because scenes of the actual victory being celebrated, with its particular *laudandus* (according to the conventions of epinician poetry) leading the triumphant revel, flank two other mythical scenes which reflect the reality of this and subsequent victories which Marathon, in the artists' conception, foretold. It is conventional enough for an epinician poet like Pindar or Bacchylides to use myth to discourse upon the present and future circumstances of his patron, and the art of these paintings would thus be typical in this regard.

> For a Pindaric myth plays something of the same role as a Homeric simile. It starts from a general similarity with the matter in hand . . . and then develops more or less independently while contriving to throw a brilliant if oblique light upon the main theme.[10]

The second panel, an *Amazonomachy* in Attica, indeed in Athens itself (which is thought to have influenced the iconography of the Parthenos shield),[11] followed by the scene of *Troy Taken* correspond to their chronological sequence in mythical time and have been interpreted as reflecting, respectively, the repulse of Xerxes' invasion of Attica and his storming of the Acropolis ten years after Marathon and his no less decisive defeat at the Eurymedon, little more than a decade later in the 460s. We read the texts of these paintings as if they were a poem, and the view from the Marathonian tomb has thus been reconstructed in Athens itself to incorporate a generation of Athenian triumph and Persian defeat. Set on either side of victories of legend, these more recent victories cast in the iconographical language of tradition, we see Marathon thus idealized,[12] its memory consecrated by this extraordinary Funeral Oration, an *epitaphios logos* of silent poetry. By participating in its construction, the Alcmaeonids could attempt to clear their reputation tarnished in the years following the battle and Cimon in particular could see in this record of his own and his father's leadership a fitting monument to the enterprise of his family. As R.E. Wycherley has well observed,

> the most extraordinary thing about these paintings is that they stood not in a secluded gallery where they could be examined by interested visitors at leisure, but in an open colonnade facing the busiest spot in Athens, where they were seen by people of all kinds going about their varied business. Plentiful evidence shows that the Poikile had the character of a *lesche* or lounge . . . where people could sit, stand, or stroll around and talk.[13]

Indeed, a *lesche* is, quite literally, a 'place to talk' and at Delphi we may still see the foundations of the banqueting hall[14] known as the Lesche of the Cnidians which was probably dedicated by their city both to acknowledge their return to the Hellenic world after years of subjection to the Persian yoke and, in the aftermath of the battle of the Eurymedon, as thanksgiving to Apollo, the god of victory and divine patron of the Athenian league, for Cimon's triumph seemed to deliver the Cnidians from the plague of Achaemenian rule. Polygnotus executed the paintings which decorated the rear wall of the lesche and, once again, we owe their description to Pausanias.[15] Both were evidently elaborate in conception: on the left (in the west) the Underworld, on the right a visitor could gaze across the sea to the east at the fall of Troy as the Greeks sailed away from the scene of their victory.

The comparison of Cimon's victory at the Eurymedon with that of Theseus' sons at Troy is even more apparent in Pausanias' description of Polygnotus' Delphic mural, for here among the vanquished Trojans we find certain names which – though they are unattested elsewhere in traditions relating to the sack of Troy – subtly remind us of Cimon's family and career. And we may see in Pausanias' record an example of 'the isolated statement', to which Macan refers, 'which serves no visible interest, but happens to survive, a fossil in an alien stratum – the most unsuspicious and serviceable of all our building materials'. Shortly after Marathon, Cimon's elder half-brother, Metiochus, had been captured by Phoenician sailors who took him to Darius. The king, however, treated him well, so Herodotus tells us, granting him a house and estate, and also a Persian wife. Among the Trojan captives Pausanias saw Metioche and expresses the opinion that Polygnotus had invented her name.[16] So too, with Eioneus, lying dead upon the Trojan plain – according to the poet Lesches, slain by Neoptolemus, Achilles' son – would Polygnotus also have intended such a reference to the son of the Greek champion at Troy who, after his father's death, brought Greek victory to its completion in the heart of the city? At any rate Eioneus cannot but reflect on Cimon's first great triumph at Eion,[17] just as the painting as a whole implies his latest and most splendid triumph at the Eurymedon, an act of 'daring resolution with which Cimon led his men, already weary from their victory over the fleet,'[18] easy though it had been, to attack the Persian enemy on land despite their numerical superiority and the fact that their position was entrenched. Wells writes of

a real Nelson touch in the desperate courage which would be

satisfied with nothing but an annihilating victory, even
though the gaining of it involved the risk of losing all that
had been already gained. . . . The victory was not unnaturally
said to surpass Salamis and Plataea rolled into one, and it
marked the highest point in the fortunes alike of Cimon and
Athens.[19]

It was an event worthy of memorial in art and song.

In introducing the paintings of the Lesche, Pausanias speaks of
the building as a place where 'people used to gather to discuss both
mythical and more earnest affairs'.[20] I do not think that Pausanias
of all people intends by this remark to diminish the significance of
myth. He may rather be reflecting the simple programme of the
paintings which associate the blaze of victory and the calm that
victory can engender with an evident declaration of our mortality,
for the *Underworld* scene is indeed a painted *Nekyia*, epic narrative
visually conceived. The Greeks envisaged immortality in a variety
of ways, but the two modes most central to their thinking were
continuity through offspring and permanence by means of 'renown
that was imperishable', *kleos aphthiton*, maintained through the
memory of future generations. In their portrayal of victory and
death, these paintings may well have aspired to the conditions of
poetry, in its expression of the same themes, not merely for
example in the encounter of Achilles and Priam, but throughout
the *Iliad* in Homer's view of life and death as Jasper Griffin has
described it.[21] Moreover, Polygnotus may have remembered
Alcinous' words to Odysseus during the pause at the centre of
Odysseus' account of his experiences in the Underworld, itself the
formal centre of Odysseus' own poem, in effect: 'in your words is a
formal beauty to match the graceful order of your ideas',[22] and
Alcinous recognizes that Odysseus is speaking truth in that he has
recovered from the bourne of forgetfulness that which is invisible
to men – since Hades is *awides* indeed – and revealed it to all. It is
hard for me not to believe that Polygnotus, knowing that quality
of poetry by which events and those involved in them were thus
made memorable sought within his own medium to achieve similar
power for his own paintings. So those fifth-century Phaeacians who
banqueted in the sight of his 'silent poetry' would themselves not
only seek to understand how particular, traditional myths were
appropriate to the recollection of their own experience,[23] but also

learn something of what Archilochus calls the *rhysmos* of mortal life, *ta spoudaiotera*, powerfully reflected in Polygnotus' great conception.

It is not important to my argument whether or not Simonides himself ever said that 'painting is silent poetry, and poetry speaking painting'. The remark nonetheless well evokes the character of the murals of the Shrine of Theseus, the Plataean temple of Athena the Warrior, the Stoa Poikile, and the Cnidian Lesche as I have just described them. On the other hand, Simonides' own preoccupation with compositional formality and its visual potential make it not unlikely that he could have held such a view, and I wish now to glance briefly at Simonides' lyric *entaphion* for the dead at Thermopylae. His epigram is among the best-known of all couplets:

> The will of Lacedaemon bade us stay
> Bring Sparta tidings still we do obey,[24]

but his lyric poem on the same theme[25] is no less remarkable. Figure 34 shows it along with my attempt to indicate the structural interdependency of its language. I do not wish even to engage the argument that the first four words are prose, merely to point out the visual quality of Simonides' poetic construction. I do not suggest that we have a shaped poem in the manner of a Simmias or George Herbert already in the fifth century, nor do I believe, with Wilamowitz, that this kind of verbal organization reflects the influence of Sophistic prose. On the contrary, the self-consciousness of early rhetorical prose in my judgement depends upon the kind of textures in which poets like Simonides and Pindar began to weave their syntax.

Simonides himself draws attention to his design by his pointed phrase *entaphion toiouton*, a burial with its altar, which, through the power of poetic memorial, 'all-conquering time' shall not diminish. The quality of this *taphos* resides in the fact that it is enshrouded within the ceremonial language of glory and praise, while, like Polygnotus' paintings in the Lesche of the Cnidians, remaining cognizant of all our mortality. This *kleos* is not merely *aphthiton*, unlike the leaves of the generations of men, incorruptible, but eternally inspired through the fertile nourishment of song, *aenaon* indeed.

I therefore believe that Simonides, himself expert at forming language in terms of the visual harmonies of a gravestone, has created this epitaph in which the structural relationship of words as well as their straightforward, grammatical syntax combine to create this *aretas megas kosmos* which, because it has been etched upon the minds of men and not on stone, will ever continue to bear testimony to Leonidas and both celebrate and be his *aenaon kleos*. The style of this *sekos* of remembrance represents a poetic counterpart of the paintings which surround the sepulchre to which Cimon delivered the Bones of Theseus who, like the dead at Thermopylae, had died far from his home.

These then are trophies of war, erected to bestow immortality upon the men who fought in them. Let us now turn to regard trophies erected by the survivors of those wars in honour of the gods and heroes who had supported them in their enterprise. I cannot begin to list here all the trophies dedicated from the spoils of battle or discuss the ways in which new cults, like that of Pan or of Artemis Eukleia with her shrine built from Marathonian spoils, came to prominence in Athens in the post-war years. We have already seen the column of the great, golden tripod at Delphi, and mentioned the bulls with which Eretria and Plataea honoured the gods. We have seen temples erected at these two cities to Apollo and Athena and must pass over particular trophies like Miltiades' helmet, Masistius' breastplate and Mardonius' sword. I would like to argue the close relationship at Athens between the new cult of Theseus and Triptolemus' return to Eleusis after the Persian withdrawal for, as Martin Nilsson had observed, Theseus 'was the heir of a settled and civilised life made possible by agriculture'.[26] But we must hasten from the city and follow the road from Athens to Delphi, laid by the 'roadbuilding sons of Hephaistos' to whom the *Eumenides'* Pythian prologue makes allusion,[27] and listen to Pindar praising Xenocrates' chariot victory in the year of Marathon.

Akousate: 'hark', cries the herald, for we are turning over
dark-eyed Aphrodite's ground or the Graces' furrows again,
on our way to the sacred navel stone of thundering earth.
There, in Apollo's valley glittering with gold, the sons of
Emmenes . . . have built themselves a treasure house of
Pythian songs which neither the winter's rain, its pitiless,
plundering army pouring from the thundering clouds, nor
wind will ever batter down and drive into the ocean's chasms,

beaten by the drift that sweeps all in its path. No, its portal (*prosopon*) standing in pure light will proclaim to mortal men the glory of your father and your family, Thrasyboulos, won in the chariot at Crisa.[28]

And so Pindar re-enacts at Xenocrates' own victory revel the actual ceremony in which his patron was crowned upon the steps of Apollo's great temple. The herald calls the victor forth, announcing his triumph, his homeland and his antecedents, and Pindar in imagination accompanies the victor up the Sacred Way and past the Treasure Houses – but my song, like Simonides' *entaphion*, so Pindar declares, is secure from the corruptibility of material wealth – to Apollo's temple itself, and we gaze with him at its *prosopon* as the victor receives his crown. Pindar's sense of place in these victory odes of his can be remarkable and I would like briefly to turn aside from Delphi and return again to the Temple of Zeus at Olympia for a view of the site active under construction, but probably before work on the temple had yet advanced much beyond the imagination of its architect and his budget council.

We join Pindar as he looks over the shoulders of the Elean Executive Committee and envisages the completed building grown from the complex ground-plan which has in every likelihood already been laid.[29] 'As when we build a shining palace, raising its portal on golden columns, so now we must make radiant the entrance to our song.'[30] Norman Gardiner was surely correct when he suggested that the prelude of Pindar's sixth *Olympian Ode* finds its source in Olympia's great architectural expectations.[31] Indeed, the whole ode, with its concentration on Iamos the Olympian visionary, his Apollonian descent and his associations with the Syracusan victor, and upon Heracles, founder of the festival and hero of the metopes, and at other points too many to mention, this ode alludes directly to the building programme of the greatest public monument of its age.

The ode is composed as a *propemptikon*, sung at Olympia probably in 468, not at Syracuse (*tonde keinon te*, line 102) to honour Agesias, victor in the least prestigious of all Olympian contests, the mule-car race, while his lord, Hiero, had finally won the Big Event, the four-horse chariot-race, but that was Bacchylides' song. Though it is not the victor that concerns us now, let us, like Pindar, begin with the gold (*khruseas*), the gold that grammatically supports the pillars (*kionas*) we shall fix (*paxomen*) in the well-walled vestibule of the *thalamos*, the sanctuary itself. *Paxomen* refers to future time, for work is just beginning (*arkhomenou ergou*, present) on ode and building alike, yet the poet looks forward at once to the final stages of construction for the *prosopon telauges* refers to the decoration of the pediment.[32] Whatever you may think of my hypothesis that the sixth *Olympian* reflects a blueprint of the Temple of Zeus, you cannot be insensitive to Pindar's fascination with the architecture of the great sanctuaries where the games were held and with the potential of architectural form as a paradigm for epinician discourse. 'We shall fix' this song as if it were a *megaron*, the shrine of a god; just look at it (cf. *thaeton*). Thus the initiation of the *ergon* in verse 3, like *hupostasantes* in verse 1, refers in typically Pindaric style, not only to his own undertaking, but also to the construction that has furnished his metaphor. For these opening lines are replete with the lexicon of architectural creativity. The literal sense of *huphistemi* is to 'lay a foundation stone' and invites us to remember Libon's technologically brilliant, if ultimately unsuccessful, attempt to secure the Temple's foundations in this earthquake-ridden land.[33]

With *euteikhei prothuroi thalamou* we approach the sanctuary itself surrounded by its gilded columns. I am less interested in the fashionable, but inapposite, metaphor that the Temple of Zeus presents us with a 'tragedy in marble' than in the poet's demand that the *megaron* become a *theatron*, an instrument of contemplation. But back to Delphi and Pindar's 'treasury'. His Ode for Xenocrates was composed, as I have mentioned, in 490. As the victor made his triumphal way towards the steps of the temple, did he pass by the Athenian Treasury, a monument which, as John Boardman has well said, was 'paid for and designed by Athens to stand in a national and politically sensitive centre of worship'?[34]

'On purely archaeological, architectural and stylistic grounds the Treasury has appeared to many scholars to date *c.* 500, and some would put it earlier.'[35] Such scholars would therefore suppose that Pindar's patron did indeed pass by the building, but the grounds which Professor Boardman cites are in open defiance of the only direct testimony antiquity has vouchsafed us for the date of the Athenian Treasury, namely, Pausanias' statement that it was dedicated 'from the spoils of the landing of Datis at Marathon'.[36] The so-called archaeological date for the Treasury is derived from

stylistic comparisons with vase-painting and contemporary sculpture, and in particular – as Beazley and Ashmole, Robertson and
Ridgway all argue in more or less detail – the sculptures at
Eretria.[37] I have already argued that caution is required in treating
the stylistic characteristics of Greek pottery like date-stamps and,
on archaeological grounds, have suggested at least the possibility of
a date in the 470s for the Temple of Apollo Daphnephorus.
Moreover, H.H. Büsing has cogently argued that architectural
parallels should also be taken into consideration, and he cites a
recently discovered anthemion-band on the inner side of the door
lintel. He compares this band with the sima of the Lesche of the
Cnidians which, as I have suggested, probably dates from the
460s. Büsing considers the painted decoration to be original and
challenges those who disagree with him to cite evidence in support
of comparable refurbishment of the building in the Early Classical
period.[38] Büsing's evidence is by no means overwhelming were
there sound reason for continuing to override Pausanias' record,
but I cannot see that any exists.

Let us therefore begin by tentatively following Pausanias'
terminus post quem of 490 and see where the hypothesis leads us. Are
we necessarily to assume that the Treasury was therefore built in
the 480s? Surely not. In any case, sculpture by Pheidias both at
Delphi and Athens is reported to have been commissioned from the
Marathonian spoils.[39] You may wish to argue that Pausanias is
once again mistaken, at least in his attribution of the sculpture to
Pheidias. But what of the Plataean Temple of Athena the Warrior
whose mural painting I suggested earlier on dated from the 450s
(p. 84)? You may point out that the paintings could have been
added later and that, in any case, the temple was probably
dedicated, at least in part, from the spoils of Plataea, as Plutarch
reports. The fact remains, however, that Pausanias declares
Marathon as the source. In these matters certainty is beyond our
reach, but I see no reason, in terms of the evidence available to us,
not to date the Treasury to the 470s, for as Beazley and Ashmole
tell us, Eretria and the Treasury belong from a stylistic standpoint
to the same period, and so does their iconography.[40]

As John Boardman remarks, the themes of the sculptural
decoration of the Treasury must have been deliberate.[41] Their
significance, if we can understand it, should tell us something
about the Athens that created the building. It is sad, then, that
uncertainty should reign about its date. I shall not discuss its

iconography in detail;[42] let me simply remind you that the east metopes depict an Amazonomachy, too lacunose for us to identify the Greek heroes who must have been involved, but I assume – and I admit the speculative nature of this assumption – that Theseus dominated the front as Heracles' battle against Geryon, the wild triform monster of the west, dominated the rear. On the north we find the Deeds of Heracles (Fig. 35), on the south those of Theseus (Fig. 36). Taken away from its topographical context, the iconography would appear to give equal weight to both heroes, if Theseus (and not Theseus together with Heracles) was indeed the protagonist at the front. The acroteria are mounted Amazons and Athena seems, appropriately enough, to have been included in the pediments, a reference, as Boardman says, 'to the dedicating state'.[43] Near the centre of the south metopes Theseus is formally received by Athens' guardian and he is dressed in the distinctive costume we have seen him wearing in a marine context (Fig. 36).

I suggest that these images are thoroughly congruent with the iconography we have come to associate so closely with Cimonian propaganda. But Heracles might seem to present a problem. In recent years, an eloquent case has been made, though its basis is entirely hypothetical, for supposing that the Peisistratids adopted Heracles as their particular hero.[44] When we see Heracles and Theseus side by side we are therefore invited to suppose some measure of rapprochement between the members of the old régime and the new democracy.[45] I suggest we should look elsewhere for our explanation of those scenes which represent Heracles and Theseus as colleagues in the same struggles. We have seen that Heracles was well established in Attica[46] before Marathon, but that the cult of Theseus was probably not introduced until the 470s, and his cult sites, unlike Heracles', are few.[47] Philochorus mentions only four. But the existence of a cult of Heracles in the sixth century does not necessarily require us to suppose public and distinctive Peisistratid patronage. Indeed, is it likely that a democracy which hated the tyrants' memory would continue to display a pre-eminent symbol of their rule while at the same time developing, against all historical verisimilitude, a cult of the Tyrannicides? Why did Heracles, unless he is nothing more than a useful turncoat, take the field at Marathon against the very army which has invaded Attica to restore that tyranny? Heracles and Theseus work together – after all, they are close kin, *suggeneis* – as old and new. Despite the Dorian associations of Heracles, his Attic cults remained active in the fifth century and I assume that Athenian artists, if their imagination transcended merely decorative convention, responded to the continued interest in this old hero.

It is, however, plausible on other grounds to suppose that the Athenian Treasury could have been built in the 470s. The Stoa of the Athenians surely represents the Athenian War memorial at Delphi. But even if the Stoa cannot be dislodged from its present chronological moorings, on what grounds is it unreasonable to suppose that Athens erected two monuments in the same decade at Delphi, after all, of a very different kind? Indeed, I suspect that the Treasury may owe its dedication to quite particular circumstances and, to understand them, let us again return to the days of the tyrants and remember that the Alcmaeonids probably suborned the sanctuary to deliver an oracle which would bring the Spartans to Athens to throw out Hippias and restore them with new powers. The Alcmaeonid Temple of Apollo has reasonably been regarded as the pay-off for this divine favour. So too, when the oracle enjoined Cimon to restore the bones of Theseus from exile on Scyros to his Athenian home and provide them with proper burial, we have seen how conveniently Delphi fostered Cimon's political ambitions in his rivalry with Themistocles (p. 69). Was the Treasury, a state building though it is – like the Shrine of Theseus, after all – the gift of Athens now once again under Alcmaeonid control, to the god who had for so long given them sanctuary[48] and supported their interests?

In the previous chapter, I mentioned the significance of the orientation of the Stoa Poikile whose spectator would face the view from the same direction as if he were standing upon the vantage point of the Marathon mound itself (p. 90). So too the entrance to the Altar of the Twelve Gods situated to the south of the Stoa and representing the zero-stone from which all Athenian mileages were computed[49] faces directly towards Olympia where the cult was first instituted.[50] The Athenian Treasury at Delphi provides an even more detailed comparison with the Stoa Poikile, for its iconography corresponds directly to the orientation of the building and its relationship to the Processional Way.

The Athenian Amazonomachy dominates the facade which faces east towards Athens and beyond it to the homeland of the Amazons. Dorian Heracles' victory over Geryon appropriately faces west as the metopes of the Treasury not only balance the Deeds of

Heracles and Theseus, Athens' new hero, but celebrate Greek victories won in both east and west over a common oriental foe. 'Let the Phoenician rue his pride at Cumae that burst into wailing for his fleet', Pindar sang to Hiero lord of Syracuse in 470.

> Such was the anguish the Syracusan king inflicted on them,
> when he hurled their youth from the swift ships into the
> waves, saving Hellas from the iron yoke of slavery. I shall
> earn the praise of Athens by singing of Salamis, and of Sparta
> by making my theme the battles beneath Cithaeron, where
> the curve-bowed Persians strove and were crushed. But when
> I come to the rivery field of Himera, I shall sing of the
> Deinomenidae, conquerors of the foe.[51]

The Athenians naturally enough gave prominence to their own hero's victory at the expense of Heracles not only by placing Theseus' triumph over his oriental foe on the front of their building, but also by relegating Heracles' Labours to the north side of the Treasury while the metopes on the south immediately proclaimed Theseus' *areta* to all who traced their steps along the Processional Way. As visitors to Delphi turned the corner from the treasuries to the south of the Sacred Way, Theseus and the new monument of Theseus' burgeoning city dominated the path before them to the north. In its own terms, the setting of the Stoa Poikile was similarly conceived and allows us to comprehend with new appreciation the way in which a Greek might interpret the intimate relationship between national achievements and their public memorial.

Let me, as a brief coda to these remarks, leave Athens and Delphi, and mainland Greece altogether, and travel west to Metaponto, 'nurse of steeds', to another sanctuary of Apollo, from which fragments of an archery contest, perhaps an Amazonomachy, and also a Centauromachy survive. According to Brunilde Ridgway, citing Adamesteanu's excavation reports,

> the temple itself dates from *c.* 530, but it was extensively
> repaired and provided with pedimental sculpture around
> 500–480. One wonders whether the lower margin given is
> perhaps more probable than the upper although the archer's
> torso recalls the Eretria pedimental sculpture. As the
> excavators point out, an Archaic date would make this carved
> set of gables unique in South Italy.[52]

Let us accept that the stylistic comparison between the Metapontine and Eretrian sculpture is valid and also take note of the anomaly of carved gables in South Italy in the sixth century. 'Einmal heisst niemals, und zweimal heisst immer.' Nonetheless, the excavators' own observations favour the view that, like Eretria, the Metapontine Sanctuary of Apollo Lykeios was dedicated in the fifth century and most likely, I suggest, as a thanks-offering for the recent victory at Himera.

And so, to cite the words with which George Rawlinson describes Herodotus' final chapter in which Cyrus repudiated Artembares' counsel that the Persians should desert their 'scant and rugged land' for 'some other country',[53] 'the end is brought back into a connexion with the beginning — the tail of the snake is curved round into his mouth; while at the same time the key-note of the whole narrative is struck, its moral suggested.'[54]

When Ernst Gombrich went 'In search of cultural history' in his Deneke Lecture for 1967, he laid particular emphasis on the influential importance of Hegel's Lectures on the philosophy of history.[55] Gombrich recalled Hegel's trinitarian theory of pre-Christian history 'where the Persians are thought . . . to represent the Father, the Greeks the Son, and the Romans the Holy Ghost, each of course', Gombrich notes, 'on a correspondingly lower plane.' For Gombrich, Hegel's conception of 'a particular national spirit' (*ein besonderer Volksgeist*) is crucial to his system, for 'world history', Hegel wrote,

> represents . . . the evolution of the awareness of the spirit of
> its own freedom. It is [the particular and determined
> *Volksgeist*] that imparts a common stamp to its religion, its
> political constitution, its social ethics, its legal system, its
> customs, but also to its science, its art and its technical
> skills. . . . Conversely, it is from the factual details present in
> history that the general character of this [distinctive
> *Volksgeist*] must be derived.[56]

Gombrich visualizes Hegel's conception as a wheel whose circumference unites the spokes radiating from the hub and goes on to express admiration for Jakob Burkhardt's application of a similar 'exegetical armature' to the study not only of the

Renaissance, but also Ancient Greece. 'Postulating the unity of all manifestations of a civilisation, [Burkhardt's] method consists in taking various elements of culture . . . and asking how they can be shown to be the expression of the same spirit.'[57]

In order to strip Hegelianism of its metaphysics, Gombrich next turns to Heinrich Wölfflin's *Renaissance und Barock*, published in 1888. 'To explain a style', Wölfflin wrote, 'cannot mean anything but to fit its expressive character into the general history of the period, to prove that its forms do not say anything in their language that is not also said by the other organs of the age.'[58] Arriving at his own day Gombrich states his alarm at the loss of assurance on the part of modern scholars regarding their perception of both 'background and foreground' in such a cultural document as Cicero's *Letters to Atticus*. 'Even classics are now threatened', Gombrich wrote only fifteen years ago, 'by that fragmentation that has long since overtaken the study of later ages',[59] a fragmentation which W.B.Stanford in 1980 declared to represent the proper 'balance of power'[60] by which alone the integrity of poetry can be protected from its quadrivial partners of history, oratory and philosophy, a quadrivium from which art and all manifestations of material culture are shockingly excluded. But Gombrich will not thus 'divide and conquer' and as his lecture was drawing to its close he lost all patience with intellectual hermits who, sealed within their particular asceticism, thus chase their own tails. And so Gombrich hopes that he has made it clear why the disappointing truth that we cannot be omniscient must on no account lead us to the adoption of an attitude of blinkered ignorance. 'We simply cannot afford this degree of professionalism if the humanities are to survive at all'.[61]

How did such a state of affairs come about? In the early nineteenth century a group of young scholars became discontented with the priority accorded to textual criticism and an annalistic approach to historical narrative. In his *Staatshaushaltung der Athener* published in 1817, August Boeckh (1785–1867), as Professor Lloyd-Jones has recently observed, 'aimed to portray a whole civilization'[62] and in his great Pindar commentary composed during the same period[63] he recognized that, as well as being transcendent poetry, Pindar's works reflected significantly upon Greek cultural history. Wilamowitz records his respect for Boeckh's contemporary, Friedrich Gottlieb Welcker, whose reading of the iconography at the Plataean Temple of Athena Areia I mentioned in the last chapter (p. 75, above), when he acknowledges that 'Welcker's equal devotion to ancient art and ancient poetry is in itself enough to make him unique'.[64] When Welcker went to Greece at the age of 57, in the words of Wilamowitz, 'he felt the presence of the gods all around him when he himself set foot on their homeland; there, they were no mere symbols, but living powers'.[65] As he climbed the hill of Colonus, he paid the tribute of a passing tear at the grave of Karl Otfried Müller who had died at Athens the year before in 1840. Müller, born in 1797, some twelve years younger than Boeckh and Welcker had, in his short life, a profound influence upon classical studies. In his doctoral dissertation, *Prolegomena to a Scientific Mythology*, written in his middle twenties, Müller had discussed the effect of ethnic heterogeneity on the cultural history of ancient Greece and already recognized something of the distinctive character of local legends. His work prepared the way for H.L. Ahrens' epoch-making analysis of the corresponding linguistic differentiation among Greek dialects at the end of the next decade which replaced Maittaire's splendid, but largely forgotten, pioneering study *Graecae linguae Dialecti* written for Westminster School just over a century before.[66] Karl Otfried Müller's most influential work, however, was his edition of the *Eumenides*, published in 1833, which propounded Welcker's notion that 'art and archaeology should contribute to the understanding . . . of a work of literature',[67] and which finally aroused the wrath of the great critic, Gottfried Hermann, against whose narrow if unsurpassed textual discipline, these younger men were reacting. Later in the century, K.J. Beloch thought fit to remark of Müller's work that he had 'dragged the ear of scholarship so deeply into the mire that it was even now scarcely possible to extricate it',[68] but in an earlier chapter I have already cited Eduard Fraenkel's judgement which fully embraces Müller's contribution:

> Henceforth no conscientious scholar was at liberty to
> comment on a Greek play without taking into account the
> monuments of art as well as the literature, or to neglect the
> relevant problems of religion, law, and political and social
> history, and the conditions of performances on the Athenian
> stage.[69]

And before he died, Hermann himself had retracted the severity of his strictures against Müller's imaginative enterprise.

The concept of *Altertumswissenschaft* derived, as Hugh Lloyd-Jones observes, 'from a fusion between the school of Boeckh and the school of Welcker and Karl Otfried Müller. . . . Such a study had to combine several different disciplines'[70] and extend the range of documentary evidence. 'The new science of comparative linguistics', Lloyd-Jones continues,

> was to throw new light upon Greek and Latin, and even upon history. Art as well as literature was to be studied with a new degree of thoroughness; both were to be studied not only for themselves, but for their social and historical significance. *Such a vast programme demanded a large measure of specialization* [my italics]. Humble scholars were content to devote their whole lives . . . to the completion of arduous but necessary tasks . . . [and they] toiled like the Nibelungen under the direction of gigantic figures like Boeckh and later Mommsen.
>
> This programme [enshrined in Boeckh's *Enzyklopädie und Methodologie der philologischen Wissenschaften*] naturally led to the adoption of a sternly realistic view of ancient society. The impulse to portray the factual and material background of ancient life had come to the historians from the romantics. . . . The view of antiquity as providing ideal standards for emulation could not longer be sustained. . . . A dry and rigid positivism crept over the work of scholars; confined each within the bounds of his narrow specialism, they became increasingly unable to see the wood of antiquity for the innumerable trees.[71]

So far as the study of Greek art is concerned, the seedlings of some of those trees were already planted by Winckelmann and how tenacious their growth has been. When he looked at a series of classicizing coins issued during the reign of Hiero the second in the late third century BC he mistook the mention of Gelon, Hiero's son, as an indication that the coinage had been issued by Gelon's namesake, the Syracusan tyrant who died in 478. Winckelmann therefore concluded that 'der Blüthe der Kunst' had already occurred by the time Xerxes invaded Greece.[72] This judgement that the classical style was in full bloom in the early fifth century undoubtedly influenced Thorwaldsen when he set about 'restoring' the Aeginetan pediments in so thoroughly a classical manner. The effect of this exercise has been not only, as Ernest Gardner recognized,[73] materially disastrous, but it reinforced, in the early nineteenth century, the aesthetic view that stylistic features which we would now regard as classical were already at home in Greece in the period prior to the Persian Wars. Such conclusions created a predisposition in the minds of the first European archaeologists to visit Greece regarding the relative antiquity of the evidence they were to find there.

And so it was when Ludwig Ross arrived in Athens in 1831 on a travelling scholarship from the Danish court to pursue at first hand his interests in Greek archaeology. He was in his mid-twenties at the time (and the nephew of a Scotsman auspiciously named Hercules). Apart perhaps from his distrust of the discipline of comparative philology, you may think that nowadays our views have little in common with his. After all, we no longer think, as he did, that the Aeginetan marbles were carved around 600 BC or that it was Cimon who built the Athenian Temple of Nike to commemorate his victory at the Eurymedon. Nevertheless, one of Ross' observations has influenced the judgement of archaeologists long beyond the mid-nineteenth century.

Ludwig Ross arrived in Athens in the immediate aftermath of the Greek war of liberation which had laid waste so much of the city. He recalled vividly the scenes of destruction which confronted him. Nothing remained that had not been touched by some recent act of savagery. Standing amid the ruined city, he thought how like it must have been when the Persians finally departed and he remembered the words of Thucydides, describing the wreckage of Athens in the wake of Xerxes' sack.[74] Invaders had come again from the east to desecrate Athenian sanctuaries and the dwellings of her citizens,[75] and in this newly shattered city, Ross began his archaeological researches.

Not long afterwards, digging on the Acropolis, he discovered various objects in a layer of burnt debris and it seemed to him as if he had come upon tokens of that earlier devastation which Thucydides had described. Thus he declared that a fragmentary red-figured plate (Fig. 37) had been a casualty of the Persian sack and the charred remains associated with it to be signs of the conflagration in which Xerxes' soldiers had destroyed the temples of Athena's citadel.[76] Ross became the first professor of Greek at the newly instituted University of Athens, but, as Wilamowitz remarks, he had been a pupil of Gottfried Hermann and, though he supplied Boeckh with carefully executed copies of inscriptions, 'his own lack of historical training gradually became very obvious'.[77] Even so, it would be entirely unreasonable for us to complain, some 150 years later, that Ross should have realized that an elaborate lamp (Fig. 38), even on present-day chronology, cannot have been made before the middle of the fifth century[78] and that an owl skyphos is scarcely older (Fig. 39).[79] Ross' identification of the flame that charred the plate as one kindled by a Persian was no more than a romantic gesture informed by what prevailing opinion about the early development of Greek art might reasonably have led him to expect. But many scholars took notice of this gesture and, by the end of the century, when Franz Studniczska[80] and Adolf Furtwängler,[81] with so much more evidence at their disposal, had articulated a general sequence of Attic pottery based on observation of its style, the Persian sack was thought to provide a crucial *terminus ante quem* for red-figured pottery comparable with Ross' plate.[82]

In view of the excavated context Ross reports, this plate obviously cannot sustain the particular interpretation he put upon it, but this conclusion need not preclude the possibility that the vessel had indeed been manufactured early in the century and only came to its archaeological resting-place together with the lamp and mug many years afterwards. Since so many other discoveries are thought to confirm that Ross was correct in principle, if not in fact, it may seem to some of you perverse of me so to privilege the discussion of this single artefact. For example, though they constitute but a small percentage of the whole, the German excavations on the Acropolis in the 1880s produced numerous sherds of burnt pottery which the excavators, explicitly acknowledging Ross' precedent,[83] interpreted in a similar manner. Although this evidence was more impressive than Ross' by weight of numbers, it is scarcely more definitive on account of the confused character of its discovery.[84] Nonetheless, it was this apparent confirmation of Ross' own conclusions that convinced Studniczska and Furtwängler, and those who have followed them, to develop the currently accepted chronology of Attic pottery and by extension that of all pre-classical Greek art. For it is by comparisons with ceramic decoration and often in defiance of epigraphic and documentary record that the dates of monumental sculpture (to mention but one example), and the structures that contained it have in large measure been derived. Since the publication of Ernst Langlotz's *Zeitbestimmung der strengrotfiguren Vasenmalerei und der gleichzeitigen Plastik* in 1920, a monograph written directly under the influence of his teacher, Studniczska,[85] few scholars – at least until recently – have seriously questioned its conclusions[86] which, at least indirectly, have determined our whole view of Greek art before the Parthenon. As a result we have come to regard so much of it, so to speak, as ahead of its time and to enforce its evidence on the reconstruction of cultural history for which alternative, corroborative testimony is so often lacking.

The words of Wentworth Dillon, fourth Earl of Roscommon, echo in my ears:

> Remember Milo's end;
> Wedg'd in that timber, which he sought to rend,

but I feel no remorse that I have no new straitjacket to offer you, to replace the one which, at times at least, reading these five chapters must surely have come to seem less reassuring than once it did. I have at least attempted, in the words of Archbishop Whately, 'to frame some canons which may furnish a standard for determining what evidence is to be received'. I hope that my reevaluation of the historical context of particular monuments and the possible intent of their iconography, along with proposals I have made about interrelating different kinds of evidence when we go in search of cultural history, will suggest not only a means of rendering obsolete some of the chronological dogma codified in Langlotz's *Zeitbestimmung*, but also – and so much more 'important – enlighten the very way in which we regard 'the grammar and harmony of pictorial art' and the role of its iconography in Greek society. I think it regrettable that Wilamowitz should have felt obliged to single out Welcker's 'equal devotion to ancient art and ancient poetry' as something so rare and I wonder how extensively he would have revised that opinion were he writing today. Yet among connoisseurs of Greek antiquity, such devotion should be a commonplace, for 'Kunstbegriff ohne Philologie ist nur einäugig'.

111

APPENDIX

THE MOTHER, THE DEMOS, AND THE DEMOSION[1]

Addressing the British Academy in October of 1942 Eduard Fraenkel spoke as follows:

> By the busy activities of many generations, the understanding of Aeschylus' plays has not only been facilitated, but in many respects dangerously obstructed. The fast-growing plant, 'fable convenue', has crept around the ancient fabric to such an extent that at many places it completely conceals the old masonry. Serious difficulties are persistently avoided or, worse, not even noticed for the sole reason that in the past some influential critic . . . improvised an arbitrary interpretation and handed it down to his successors, who in their turn took the solution for granted.[2]

With Fraenkel's stricture as epigraph, let us consider two propositions nowadays commonplace not only among students of Greek religion, but also those interested in the administration of democratic institutions at Athens. For it is widely agreed that the cult of the Phrygian Mother, Cybele, was introduced into Athens' civic centre in the early years of Cleisthenic democracy, and political historians tell us that, while administering both state and empire, Athens continued without a formal, centralized public archive of any kind – a Public Records Office, I shall call it – until the end of the fifth century.[3] However unrelated these two propositions may at first sight appear, the evidence said to favour the one in my judgement bears directly on the other. And to focus our discussion, let us revisit a small building which once stood on the west side of the Athenian Agora, identified in Fig. 40 as the 'Temple of Meter'.

First, let us establish some archaeological bearings: the

excavators agree that the structure in question was erected, in
Homer Thompson's words, at 'a date . . . very shortly after' the
Bouleuterion immediately to its south and indeed formed part of
the same building project.[4] Both buildings were aligned upon the
Great Drain constructed, so its stratigraphy implies, before the
Council Chamber, but again as part of the same programme of
public works, conceived with a view to a more commodious and
monumental Agora. The foundations of our building – the one
directly north of the Council Chamber – originally supported a
structure with a porch *in antis*, a design which scholars without
exception have taken to reflect that of a small temple. And only
Charles Picard[5] and J.S. Boersma[6] have, to my knowledge,
questioned the initial and now standard view that the American
team had excavated a temple dedicated to the Mother of the Gods.
In publishing these buildings on the west side of the Agora in
1937, Homer Thompson dated the Old Bouleuterion, and hence
the building to the north, to the early years of Cleisthenes'
constitutional reforms, and nowadays most scholars, except
apparently Professor Thompson himself, remain content with this
judgement.[7]

Homer Thompson's observations had an immediate impact on
the historiography of Greek religion. Cybele had, of course,
already been recognized elsewhere on the Greek mainland, but
evidence predating the last quarter of the fifth century was
restricted to Pindar's poetry.[8] The citizens of Laconian Acriae
might well boast to Pausanias[9] that theirs was Cybele's oldest
Peloponnesian sanctuary, but we cannot say, even were the claim
true, how old that may be.[10] At Athens, however, the only
Mother for whom any documentary evidence exists prior to the
420s dwelt across the Ilissus at Agrae – and her cult was evidently
associated, not with the Asiatic Mother and her familiar
appurtenances of lions and castanets, but with the Lesser Mysteries
of Demeter.[11] So when and how was the cult of Cybele introduced
to Athens? The question is not a trivial one since that divinity has
such patently oriental connections that her liturgical presence at
Athens is by no means a matter of course. We turn for guidance to
Martin Nilsson's *Geschichte der griechischen Religion* published shortly
after Thompson's study of the west side of the Agora. Citing
Thompson's work Nilsson reports an Athenian tradition (though
not attested before Julian) that, during a time of plague, the
Athenians consulted Delphi to learn the cause of their misfortune.

The Pythia reminded them that they had once maltreated a mendicant priest of the Phrygian Mother whom they should accordingly propitiate. So the Athenians built her a temple and introduced the practice of her cult. And when was this Gallos or *metragyrtes* thus avenged? At the end of the sixth century, so Nilsson thought.[12] And why did Nilsson think that? Because – and only because – he accepted Thompson's interpretation of the function of that building in the Agora as a Cleisthenic Temple of the Mother.

No matter that, at this very period, these same Athenians were about to incinerate, however accidentally, the great house of that same divinity across the sea at Sardis. No matter that otherwise we hear no whisper, catch no glimpse of Cybele's presence at Athens before the 420s – by contrast with the last years of the sixth century, a decade following a plague worthy of doxographers. No matter that, as the authors of *Agora 14* report, from the so-called temple itself, 'no trace of a cult statue or its base survives'.[13] Nonetheless, R.E. Wycherley writes that our building 'can be identified confidently as the Metroon' and that from the archaic period onwards, 'there was a very close association between the cult of the Mother of the Gods and the Bouleuterion'[14] – though one is a monument to the preservation of political order while the other is associated, at least in some of her epiphanies, with dire acts of liturgical excess. Though we may readily understand the loss of the cult statue itself, there remains no trace of its base, no epigraphic or literary means of identification, but a temple notwithstanding, and a temple with a collar: 'I belong to Mother'.

What has breathed such vitality into these stones that, so mute, they thus speak? And speak so loud that scholars from W.K.C. Guthrie to Walter Burkert accept Nilsson's reconstruction of Cybele's Athenian advent;[15] or that Joan Haldane can write in *Phoenix* that the dissemination of Mother-worship with Athens as its epicentre reflects one of the most prominent religious tendencies in early fifth-century Greece?[16] Indeed, G.P. Stevens was so persuaded by our modern sense of a neighbourly relation between civic Council and Mother's cult that he considered the celebrated 'Lioness lintel' part of a window built into the Old Bouleuterion *c.* 450, an iconographic echo of the leonine attributes of the goddess next door.[17] Such then, albeit selectively, is our 'fable convenue' which after fifty years has indeed grown so fast and tenaciously around the ancient fabric that, in my judgement and

114

Eduard Fraenkel's metaphor, 'the old masonry' is by now completely concealed.

So let us begin again, with some questions. Was the building on the southwest corner of the Athenian Agora, immediately north of the Old Bouleuterion, originally constructed as a Metroon? If not, was it ever, subsequent to its original foundation, so used? Indeed, was it, so far as we know, in antiquity ever so called? It may seem depressing, but under the circumstances of our knowledge of fifth-century Athens, by no means unusual, to be obliged to report that no direct evidence exists on which to base secure replies to any of these questions. Put more positively, unless you weigh rhetoric over substance, no evidence exists which requires the hypothesis that the building was ever designed or used as a Metroon, or was ever so called until the 1930s.

In order to understand why so many scholars have supposed otherwise, let us for the moment leave the fifth century and look at the relevant structures first as they stood in the time of Demosthenes, Aeschines and Lycurgus, and then let us revisit the scene with Pausanias for by then the architecture of the area will have undergone substantial remodelling. Now we know that the name 'Metroon' was bestowed consecutively upon at least two buildings in the southwest corner of the Agora, namely, the building to which I have been referring, from a fifth–century standpoint, as the Old Bouleuterion and a later structure, built probably in the third quarter of the second century BC, the foundations of which encompass those of both the Old Bouleuterion and the building *sub judice* to the north.[18] The Old Council Chamber, which Pericles would of course have called 'Bouleuterion' *simpliciter*, was replaced by a new one, built to the west of it, probably before the end of the fifth century. At any rate the New Council Chamber was certainly in place before our earliest testimony denominating its functional predecessor as 'Metroon'.[19] And so, when Aeschines says in 330: 'In the metroon beside the Bouleuterion, it is possible to see what gift you gave to those who brought back the demos from exile at Phyle'[20] he is speaking of the two Council Chambers, old and new. But when Pausanias visits Athens in the second century AD and records the shrine of the Mother of the Gods near the Bouleuterion of the Five Hundred,[21] he refers to the rectangular, Hellenistic Metroon or at least *pars pro toto* to the hieron of the Mother within it, whose cult–statue was housed in the second cella from the southern end through which the visitor could gain access to the eastern entrance of the New Bouleuterion.

The fifth-century Council Chamber was renamed Metroon – our evidence dates from the second quarter of the fourth century – in part to distinguish it from the Council Chamber which had replaced it and also for the reason that it was now associated with the cult of the Mother and probably housed the cult-statue to which both Pausanias and Pliny refer. Pausanias gives the statue to Pheidias,[22] Pliny to his pupil, Agoracritus.[23] Modern opinion reasonably favours Pliny's attribution, for though we can no longer see the original – unless one believes with Rhys Carpenter that she may reside in Boston[24] – several small marble votives found in the Agora allow us to reconstruct the type and we are plainly dealing, from an iconographic standpoint, with the Asiatic Mother, with her lions and tympana.[25] Even though these putative copies suggest an original by Agoracritus rather than Pheidias, it would be hazardous to insist on an exact date for the statue itself, but plausible to attribute it to the last quarter of the fifth century. This statue at any rate could not have stood in our building, especially if, as Professor Thompson first believed, that building was destroyed by the Persians in 480. We have no evidence of any earlier statue which Agoracritus might have replaced. We also know a fair amount about the function of this fourth-century Metroon. It served as Athens' Public Records Office and we may suppose that these state documents were now stored under the Mother's special tutelage. But such an association between Bouleuterion and Metroon in fourth-century Athens, comprehensible enough in the cultural conditions of the age, neither requires nor entitles us to reconstruct a comparable, but potentially anachronistic, relationship for the early fifth century between the Old Bouleuterion and the building adjacent to it. Following that same analogy one might as well think of that building as a Public Records Office, but such a possibility, never seriously raised, has been flatly denied, for example, by E. Posner in his influential study of *Archives in the Ancient World* in which he asserts that 'the original Metroon had nothing to do with the preservation of archives'.[26]

When we consider the Hellenistic Metroon we find it divided into two main sectors united by a broad colonnade facing east towards the Agora. The southern sector, subdivided into three rectangular rooms, was constructed over the square of the Metroon, *quondam* Council Chamber, and the northern half covered not only the area of our building, but also the space between it and the Old Bouleuterion. Of the three southern rooms, the central one apparently housed the Mother whose statue faced towards her altar situated outside the building, in front of the colonnade. The two rooms flanking this hieron are thought to have been used for the storage and consultation of state archives. The large northern room seems to have been a two-storey structure which may well have served both as the official residence of the director of the archive and as the permanent depository of state documents – the stacks, so to speak, as opposed to the reference and reading rooms to the south, for Wycherley and Thompson have suggested that the whole building was conceived under the influence of the new, Pergamene library, the one presided over by Athena, the other – in a nice chiastic irony – by the Hellenized epigone of the Asiatic Mother.[27]

If indeed this Hellenistic Metroon contained at its northern end an official residence and an archival deposit, then perhaps we should wonder, in terms of the principle of functional continuity, if the building upon which it was superimposed – our building – might not have been similarly employed in the fifth century, if not as an official residence, at least as the formal office for preserving the records of Boule and Ecclesia. But why in a temple? But is our building a temple? Remember, we know of no late archaic cult-statue and no trace exists of a statue base. Perhaps the builders of the Hellenistic Metroon destroyed all trace of such evidence, but evidence there is none. So let us try a new line of reasoning: no statue, no base, no evidence of cult, no temple. Not all buildings constructed with a porch distyle *in antis* are temples, some are Treasuries – compare, for example, the Athenian Treasury at Delphi – and a Treasury not only requires no cult image, but represents an apt architectural prototype for a political strong-box enshrining the documentary record of democratic government. I therefore suggest that the so-called late archaic Temple of Meter was not only topographically adjacent to the Old Bouleuterion as part of the same building programme, but also functionally adjunct to it, constructed to serve as a Public Records Office supervised by the official, known later at least as the *grammateus tes boules*.

From the standpoint of Athenian cultural history at this period, I find such a juxtaposition more plausible than that of Council

Chamber and Metroon and do not regard Cybele's presence on a Delphic frieze or in Pindar's poetry sufficient grounds for supposing that her cult was widely disseminated in mainland Greece in the first half of the fifth century. On the mainland there is ample testimony for Athenian interest in such exotic and indeed oriental cults in the social crises of the Peloponnesian War. And before the publication of Nilsson's *Geschichte*, W.S.Ferguson and E.R.Dodds had eloquently accounted for the arrival in Athens of such divinities as Sabazius, Bendis – the Great Mother of Thrace – and Cybele herself, not to mention Asclepius' 'medical reptile', as reflecting the religions of emergency, hastily yet fervently embraced in times of desperate peril.[28] At this period too, the Ionian recognition of Artemis and Cybele, *potniai theron* both, as major civic deities no doubt contributed significantly to the naturalization of the Asiatic Mother in a political role and her Hellenizing translation as Rhea, the mother of the Olympian pantheon. And so to the Mother of the Gods was now assigned the task of guarding the documents of state by reference to which constitutional order was maintained and the intrusion of wilder influences kept at bay.

If we reject the conventional view of the building just north of the Old Bouleuterion, what can be said of the new function I have attributed to it? Moreover, when was it built and who built it? In his account of 'State Documents in Archaic Athens' Ronald Stroud writes of 'considerable archival activity at Athens'[29] earlier in the fifth century, but endorses Alan Boegehold's 'convincing demonstration that a centralized archive was not established until its last decade'. Boegehold, however, was puzzled by the frequent occurrence of the phrase, *en toi demosioi*, and inquires why orators speak of transferring documents from the Bouleuterion *eis to demosion*.[30] I suggest that *demosion* was a term used to describe the *grammateion*, the archival annex I have reconstructed in which the *grammateus tes boules* or his official predecessor placed state documents on permanent file. This functionary has a fifth century counterpart at Elis in the person of Patrias, known epigraphically as *ho gropheus*,[31] and we may wonder whether Dörpfeld's Bouleuterion at Olympia[32] does not owe its unusual design, odd for a meeting place, to a similar use as the Olympic archive.[33] At Athens, it was perhaps not so much, as Boegehold argues, a new attitude towards record-keeping and archival centralization[34] (though both factors were probably at work), but the proliferation of state documents which led the Athenians towards the end of the century to recognize the need for a greatly expanded record office. The construction of a new Council Chamber allowed for its functional predecessor to meet these needs, needs which could no longer adequately be served within the confined quarters of the original *demosion*, if indeed, contrary to general opinion, that building was still standing.

I think perhaps it may have been, but this conjecture depends in part upon a question: when was it built? In relative terms, 'very shortly after' the Old Bouleuterion. So what is the date of the Council Chamber? The excavators originally judged the building to be Cleisthenic despite the apparent lack of evidence for Persian destruction, but Homer Thompson has recently drawn attention to the fire-damaged blocks, re-used in the building's inner foundations which he reasonably identifies as a sign of the Persian sack, supposing that the builders concealed in the Council Chamber's foundations usable, if damaged, masonry belonging to some earlier structure which the Persians had indeed set on fire. Thompson associates this new building with the landmark reforms of Ephialtes which gave the Athenian Council and Assembly sweeping new prerogatives.[35] As for the building to the north, the excavators simply assumed (because they thought it was a temple) that the Persians must have destroyed it, though the remains of the building itself yield no trace of such destruction. On the other hand, if the building was erected as an archival annex to the Bouleuterion around 460 or soon afterwards, we can see why such evidence is lacking. And we may also be led to a new understanding of Anaximenes' testimony that 'Ephialtes transferred the laws of Solon from up on the Acropolis to the Bouleuterion and the Agora' for all to see.[36] With the diminution of the archons' power, Athenian citizens clearly enjoyed new standards of public accountability and accessibility. 'The enhanced role of the Demos brought about by Ephialtes' reforms' may well have been reflected, as Thompson suggests, as a material corollary, in a programme for the construction of a new administrative centre.[37] The Tholos, built to house the council presidents – and remember that no evidence places the prytany-system before this period – the Tholos stood appropriately in front of the entrance to the Council Chamber (Fig. 6). At its rear, a Public Records Office housed the archives of the newly empowered democracy, and other administrative structures in or near the Agora can now, according to Professor

Thompson, be associated with the same building programme of civic offices in a decade when Athens centralized the administration of her Empire.[38]

Who guided this ambitious project? With Ephialtes dead and Cimon ostracized, Pericles becomes the most likely candidate to have carried forward in word and deed the reforms attributed to Ephialtes. As Myronides and the other generals swayed the Assembly on the basis of their military experience, Pericles may well have taken his opportunity to oversee the construction of new public accommodations to meet the needs of constitutional reforms in the achievement of which he had so closely participated. In reflecting upon his initial reconstruction of the history of these democratic buildings, Homer Thompson recalls that 'the excavators were driven to rely largely on *historical probability* [my italics] in proposing even a tentative date for [their] first period' and they took the democratic reforms of Cleisthenes to provide 'the most probable occasion'.[39] Now that archaeological evidence has persuaded Professor Thompson to revise these initial impressions, we need no longer assume that Athens' civic centre sprang fully furbished from the head of Cleisthenes, but can attribute it instead to the period when Athenian democracy 'came of age' in the political reorganization which indeed consolidated the demos in its power. And, as a consequence, a far more convincing 'historical probability' has surely been attained, for as Felix Jacoby opined in *Atthis*, the administration of state and empire 'could not have been achieved without records and the records had to be kept somewhere. Actually the place is of no importance'.[40] Perhaps not, but I thought you might like to know where it was, all the same — and if you are wondering why its possible discovery has been so long delayed, then add 'fable convenue' to that well-known aetiology of symptoms in the Hippocratic treatise on 'The Sacred Disease': 'if the patient imitate a goat, if he roar or suffer convulsions in his right side, they say that the Mother of the Gods is to blame.'[41]

NOTES

1 GREEK ART IN AN HISTORICAL SETTING

1 Aeschylus, *Persians* 348–9.
2 Herodotus 7, 141.
3 Jameson 1962, 312.
4 Wells 1923, 136.
5 ibid., 126.
6 ibid., 125–6.
7 cf. Nylander 1970, 15–16.
8 cf. Barron 1980, 8, n. 54; Vickers 1987 [1984].
9 For these events, see Lewis 1977, 83–107.
10 Francis 1980, 53–4.
11 Timotheus, *Persians* 188–95 Page.
12 Herodotus 9.80.
13 Herodotus 9.82.2; cf. Vickers 1989 [1984].
14 Gauer 1968; D.B.Thompson 1956.
15 e.g. Hoffmann 1961. Fig. 1 illustrates the rhyton Leningrad, Hermitage Museum, inv. B 1818, ARV^2 382, 188.
16 Tuchelt 1962.
17 Von Gall 1977, 1979.
18 Plutarch, *Pericles* 13.5.
19 Broneer 1952.
20 D.B. Thompson 1956.
21 cf. LSJ, *s.v. skiadeion*; for a qualification, see Davies 1981, 290–1.
22 Schmidt 1953, pl. 75.
23 Rhodes 1972, 16–30, 203; 1982 ibid. and 305–6; Rhodes 1981, 317.
24 Stewart 1979, 134.
25 Gardner 1926, vii.
26 Boardman 1982, 3.
27 ibid., 3–4.

28 Stewart 1979, 133.
29 Sextus Empiricus, *Pyrr. Hyp.* 1.10.
30 Rome, Conservatori Museum, inv. 980; Helbig 1966, No. 1508.
31 Both in the Chalcis Museum.
32 Robertson 1975, 164.
33 cf. Redfield 1975.
34 Boardman 1982, 9, n. 29. '490' was subsequently said to have been a misprint for '499': Boardman 1984, 161, n. 1.
35 Or thirty–odd if 490 was indeed a misprint.
36 Herodotus 5.97.
37 Herodotus 5.101.
38 Kourouniotis 1900.
39 Auberson 1968, 24.
40 Coulton 1979, 102–4.
41 It has been maintained that this was indeed the case (Boardman 1984, 161–2).
42 e.g. Boardman 1984, 161–2.
43 Herodotus 2.112.
44 cf. Francis and Vickers 1983.
45 Herodotus 6.101,119.
46 Herodotus 8.1,46.
47 Herodotus 9.28,31.
48 cf. Francis and Vickers 1983, 52, n. 30.
49 Mallwitz 1972, 94; Francis and Vickers 1983, 52, n. 32.
50 Meritt *et al.* 1939–53, 1, 270–1; 3, 57 and 99, n. 1.
51 Myres 1953, 195.
52 Boardman 1978a, 156.
53 Boardman 1982, 9.
54 Gomme 1952, 78; 1962, 30.
55 Herodotus 8.20.
56 For the principles underlying these assumptions, see Ashmole 1972 and Coulton 1977.
57 Auberson and Schefold 1972, 115.
58 Gauer 1980.
59 e.g. the red–figure amphora in the Louvre, Inv. G. 197: ARV^2 238, 1; Francis 1980, 69–70; Boardman 1982, 15–16. See Fig. 28.
60 Myres 1953, 203.
61 Herodotus 6.99.
62 Herodotus 8.66.
63 Herodotus 8.112.1–2.
64 Thucydides 1, 98, 3; Meiggs 1973, 69–70.
65 Boardman 1978a, 185.
66 Contrast Herodotus 6.112 (on Marathon): 'Until that day even to

hear the name of the Medes was a terror (*phobos*) to the Greeks' with Aeschylus *Persians* 391: 'Fear (*phobos*) was in the hearts of all the barbarians'.

67 Ridgway 1977, 7.
68 Ridgway 1977, 316, n. 15.
69 Pausanias 10.11.4.
70 Boardman 1982, 4.
71 Dunbabin 1949, 141.
72 Herodotus 3.57–8; Francis and Vickers 1983. [The editor has suggested elsewhere (Vickers 1985b) that the building now generally known as the 'Siphnian' Treasury may have been mis-identified. While he was generally in favour of these arguments, E.D. Francis had reservations regarding the suggestion made (ibid.) that Euripides' *Erechtheus* was performed in 412. These would, one hopes, have been removed in the light of Vickers 1989.]
73 Harrison 1965, 5.
74 Herodotus 5.102.
75 Timotheus, *Persians* 98–139.
76 Aeschylus, *Persians* 447 ff.; Herodotus 8.95.
77 Pindar, *Pythian* 3, 78.
78 Nilsson 1941, 687, n. 3.
79 Thompson 1937.
80 Dodds 1951, 193–4.
81 Thompson 1937, 140.
82 Rhodes 1972, 16–30; 16–30 and 305–6 in 1982 edition; Rhodes 1981, 317.
83 Thompson 1937, 222.
84 Thompson 1982, 136–7; cf. 1978, 1981, 345–6; Rhodes 1981, 522.
85 Thompson 1937.
86 See further, Appendix pp. 112–20, and Francis and Vickers 1987.
87 Posner 1972, 103.
88 Boegehold 1972, 29.
89 Thompson 1981, 346.
90 After Francis and Vickers 1988, Fig. 7.
91 Ehrenberg 1973, 443.
92 Meiggs, 1973, 156.
93 *Athenaion Politeia* 7, 1.
94 Plutarch, *Pericles* 13, 1.

2 IMAGES OF GLORY AND THE ART OF POWER

1 Rhodes 1972, 16–30; also 305–6 in 1982 edn; Rhodes 1981, 317.
2 Thompson 1940.

3 Shear 1978.
4 Thompson 1982, 137.
5 See further, Appendix, pp. 112–20.
6 *Athenaion Politeia* 7.1.
7 Thompson 1982, 137.
8 *Agora Guide* 1963, 52; cf. *Agora Guide* 1954, 41.
9 *Agora Guide* 1954, 40.
10 Schmidt 1939, 9–15, fig. 7; 1953, 210, figs 82–3.
11 Francis and Vickers 1988.
12 Aeschylus, *Persians* 240; cf. Herodotus 7.144.
13 Thompson 1982, 136.
14 Hughes 1980, 367.
15 Macleod 1982, 54, with Griffin 1983a, 4.
16 Herodotus 5.102.
17 Simonides fr. 13 Page; Huxley 1978, 234.
18 Devambez 1976; Ridgway 1974.
19 Boardman 1982, 13.
20 Herodotus 5.99–103.
21 Boardman 1982, 13.
22 *FGH* 70 F 9.
23 [Gill 1988, however, shows that even on the traditional chronology, the pottery found beneath the terrace on which the temple of Aphaia was built provides a *terminus post* for the construction of the temple of 480.]
24 Meiggs 1973, 52, with n. 2, citing Thucydides 1.95.4.
25 Meiggs 1973, 51.
26 MacDowell 1960, 121.
27 cf. Ridgway 1977, 212, n. 37.
28 Williams 1982, 65.
29 Blakesley 1854, 2, 383, citing F. Thiersch in Boettiger 1820–5, 1, 137.
30 Wade–Gery 1952, 88–94; but note G. Kirk's review (Kirk 1954, 190–1), and Pherecydes' Cimonian genealogy (Huxley 1973, 141).
31 Herodotus 8.121.
32 Bowra 1964, 298.
33 Finley 1966, 9.
34 Pindar, *Isthmian* 5, 48–50, tr. Jebb. On *anaritmos*/unnumbered, cf. the concept of 'horde' in both Aeschylus' *Persians* and Herodotus.
35 Herodotus 8.122.
36 Pindar, *Paean* 6 (fr. 52f, Snell/Maehler) 117–21.
37 As an image of St Elmo's fire, the emblem of rescue for sailors facing shipwreck (cf. the imagery of Pindar, *Isthmian* 5, 46 ff.), already used in the context of the ship of state by Alcaeus (34 Page).
38 Blakesley 1854, 2, 383.

39 Meiggs 1973, 51.
40 See, however, Gill 1988.
41 Jebb 1882, 178.
42 Boardman 1978a, 156.
43 Wilamowitz [1927] 1982, 164.
44 Herodotus 8.99.
45 Griffin 1983b, 398.
46 Stanford 1980, 123.
47 Macleod 1982, 144.
48 Fraenkel 1950, 1, 50–1.
49 Zuntz 1955, 79.
50 Aeschylus, *Persians* 824–6.
51 ibid., 821–2.
52 *Iliad* 2, 100–108, cf. Thuc. 1, 9, 4. Note that in the Iliadic passage, Hephaestus first passes the sceptre to Zeus who then orders Hermes as courier to give it to Pelops. In the *Agamemnon*, the order is altered perhaps so that symbolic prominence may be given to Hermes' role as messenger in the beacon sequence.
53 Fraenkel 1950, 2, 161.
54 Parke 1977, 172–3.
55 ibid.
56 Aeschylus, *Agamemnon* 55.
57 At Aeschylus, *Agamemnon* 312–14; cf. Fraenkel 1950, 2, 166–9; Quincey 1963, 119–20.
58 Though this was not the term itself, according to Frisk 1954–72, 3, 16, cf. 1, 7–8. Cf. Fries 1903, 169–70; 1904, 117–21 and references in Frisk *loc.cit.*
59 For discussion, see Lewis 1977, 56–7 (with references in nn. 51 and 52, esp. to Riepl 1913, in n. 51, who includes a full account of the ancient evidence); also Cook 1983, 106–9 (esp. 108), 245.
60 Herodotus 9.3.1.
61 cf. Burn 1984, 499.
62 cf. *de Mundo* 398A. For the use of the *angareion* and beaconing together, cf. Herodotus 8.98, Cleomedes 2.1.21, Xenophon *Cyropedia* 8.6.18, *Hellenica* 6.2.33–4.
63 Diodorus 11.61.
64 cf. Nepos, *Miltiades* 7; Dio Cassius 46.36. On signalling by beacons, see esp. Polybius 10.43–7 (with Walbank 1967, 258) and Diodorus 19.57.
65 Herodotus 7, 41. Cf. D.B. Thompson 1956, 287; Francis 1980, 56–7, n. 11.
66 cf. Fraenkel 1950, 2, 417.
67 Bacon (1961), 102–3.
68 22 April 1983, 398.

69 ibid.
70 Xenophanes 11–12 D.–K.; Pindar *Olympian* 1.29; *Nemean* 9.103–4.
71 cf. Francis 1980, 62.
72 Finley (1966), 1.
73 Aeschylus, *Agamemnon* 1381–7 (tr. Fagles).
74 Boston, Museum of Fine Arts, Inv. 63.1246; *Para.* 373, 34 *quater*.
75 'Philologie ohne Kunstbegriff ist einaügig': Bapp (1921) 61.
76 Pindar, *Nemean* 5, 20.
77 Naples, Archaeological Museum, Inv. Heydemann 3253; Cornford 1907, 194–7; Schmidt 1960; Francis 1980, 84–6. Fig. 8 is taken from Furtwängler/Reichold 1904, pl. 88.
78 Porphyry, *On Abstinence* 2, 142.
79 Hinks 1939, 65, n. 5.
80 Aelian, *True History* 12.62; Brunn 1881, 107.
81 Cornford 1907, 195; Herodotus 7.10.
82 Aeschylus, *Persians* 107–14.
83 Edinburgh, Royal Museum of Scotland, Inv. 1887.213; *ARV²* 364, 46.
84 Hamburg, Museum für Kunst und Gewerbe, Inv. 1981.173; Hornbostel 1982, 109–12.
85 On the semantic range of this word, see Francis 1975, esp. 54, n. 24.
86 Dover 1978, 105.
87 Naples, Museo Nazionale, Inv. 2422; *ARV²* 189, 74 and Louvre, Inv. G 152, *ARV²* 369, 1.
88 Staatliche Museen, Inv. 2293, *ARV²* 370, 10.
89 Herodotus 9.11.
90 Aeschylus, *Persians* 816–17, 823–4, tr. Morshead.
91 Paris, Cabinet des Médailles, Inv. 573, *ARV²* 417, 1.

3 WORD AND CEREMONY

1 Some of the ideas in this chapter first took form in a paper ('Political poetry and political painting 480–460 BC') I gave with Michael Vickers at the Cambridge Philological Society in October 1980.
2 cf. Davie 1982, 32.
3 Brommer 1982, 74.
4 Jacoby 1949, 395; Schefold 1946, 67.
5 Sourvinou–Inwood 1971, 97–8.
6 Fraenkel 1942, 249.
7 ibid., 250–1.
8 Barrett 1964, 3.
9 ibid.
10 Pausanias 10.11.4.

11 Boardman 1982, 4.
12 Sourvinou–Inwood 1971, 98.
13 Bacchylides 17 Snell.
14 Bacchylides 18 Snell.
15 cf. Francis and Vickers 1984.
16 Wilamowitz 1937 [1925], 75.
17 Jacoby 1949, 395.
18 Boardman 1982, 1.
19 Plutarch, *Theseus* 29.
20 Wells 1923, 134.
21 Plutarch, *Theseus* 6.
22 Nilsson 1953, 745.
23 Wells 1923, 134.
24 Wells 1923, 131–3.
25 Herodotus 8.132.
26 Herodotus 7.185.
27 Wells 1923, 133.
28 Plutarch, *Theseus* 36; cf Barron 1972, 20.
29 cf. Davie 1982.
30 Pausanias 1.17.2.
31 Wycherley 1959, 155.
32 Barron 1972, 22.
33 ibid., 21–2.
34 Barron 1972; Robertson 1975, 256.
35 Paris, Louvre, Inv. G. 341, ARV^2 601, 22.
36 Munich, Museum antiker Kleinkunst, Inv. 2640, ARV^2 402, 22.
37 Woodford 1974, 160.
38 ibid., 161, n. 20.
39 Nilsson 1951, 33.
40 Tomlinson 1980.
41 Pausanias 10.25.1.
42 Parke 1977, 81–2.
43 Pausanias 1.17.6.
44 Pausanias 1.18.1.
45 Merkelbach 1973.
46 Robert 1898.
47 Kenyon 1897, 176.
48 Jebb 1905, 233–4.
49 Siewert 1977, 109–10.
50 Perhaps, though, these tokens taken together represent a synthesis between the first arrival of Theseus from Troezen and his present (and final) return home from Scyros.
51 Davies 1971, 306f.
52 Barron 1980.

53 Raubitschek 1955, 288–99, n. 13.
54 Barron 1980, 1, 5.
55 *FGH* 3 F 149; Barron 1980, 1, 5.
56 From Huxley 1973, 141.
57 Plutarch, *Theseus* 35.4.
58 Herodotus 5.65; Nilsson 1953, 748.
59 Barron 1980, 5, n. 4.
60 Plutarch, *Cimon* 14.
61 Plutarch, *Cimon* 4.6.
62 Barron 1980, 2.
63 Hammond 1982, 83–7.
64 Paris, Louvre, Inv. G. 195, *ARV*^{2} 381, 174.
65 Bacchylides 17 Snell.
66 Segal 1979, 31.
67 ibid., 34; cf. Nagy 1973, 145–8.
68 Segal 1979, 34–5.
69 e.g. Burnett 1984, 165, thinks that Segal's analysis 'may be a bit strong'.
70 Plutarch, *On the Glory of Athens* 3.
71 Pausanias 1.17.2–3.
72 New York, Metropolitan Museum, Inv. 53.11.4 and 1970.46, *ARV*^{2} 406, 7; Bothmer 1970, 83.
73 Parry in Fagles, Bowra, and Parry 1961, 17.
74 Lines 31 and 54: relevant here, perhaps, is the Phoenician component of the Persian fleet (Aesch., *Persians* 410), as well as fifth-century awareness of Minos' sea-power (Herodotus 3.122). See too Barron 1980, n. 47.
75 Paris, Louvre, Inv. G. 104, *ARV*^{2} 318, 1.
76 Latte 1968, 708–9.
77 Barron 1980, 4.
78 Barron, ibid., and 8, n. 53.
79 ibid., and 8, n. 54.
80 Herodotus 3.122.
81 Plutarch, *Cimon* 9.1.
82 cf. Sourvinou-Inwood 1979.
83 Ostby 1980; Doumas 1963, pl. 327c.
84 Parke 1977, 80–3.
85 See, however, Shapiro 1982, 296.
86 Boardman 1982, 1.
87 Parke 1977, 82.
88 cf. Sourvinou–Inwood 1971, 109, n. 69.
89 Jeffery 1965, 42.
90 Aeschylus, *Persians* 765.
91 Sourvinou–Inwood 1979, 29–47.

92 Wells 1923, 137, citing Aristotle, *Politics* 3.7.3.
93 Philostratus, *Lives of the Sophists* 2.1.545–6; *IG* 14.1389.1.30–33; cf. Barron 1980, 6, n. 22.
94 Wycherley 1978, 155.

4 'SILENT POETRY'

1 Wells 1923, 135.
2 Pausanias 3.3.6; cf. Herodotus 1.67–9 (with Rawlinson 1875, *ad loc.*).
3 Plutarch, *Cimon* 5.
4 Pausanias 10.14.3.
5 Thucydides 1.20.
6 *FGH* 239 A 54. Brunnsåker 1971, 43; [for reservations concerning the reliability of the Parian Marble, see Vickers 1985a, 30; if these are correct, a date for the Tyrannicides in the 460s is possible].
7 cf. Huxley 1978, 244.
8 Boston, Museum of Fine Arts, Inv. 1970.567; Kinzl 1978, pl. 2.
9 Hyperides 2 *Against Philip* 3.
10 Rhodes 1981, 289, n. 28.
11 Plutarch, *Themistocles* 1; Simonides, fr. 122 Page.
12 Boardman 1982, 21.
13 Barron 1972, 39.
14 Alternatively, we might consider the possibility that the Tyrannicides fought 'side by side' rather than 'back to back'.
15 Barron, 1972, 40.
16 Westlake 1936.
17 cf. British Museum, Inv. E. 84; ARV^2 729, 4.
18 Munich, Museum antiker Kleinkunst, Inv. 2044, *ABV* 146, 21.
19 Paris, Louvre, Inv. G 197; ARV^2 238, 1.
20 Boardman 1982, 16; cf. Hölscher 1973, 30–1, 233, nn. 62–6; Francis 1980, 64–5; 69–70.
21 Bacchylides 3.
22 Naples, Inv. Astarita 428; ARV^2 242, 77.
23 Boardman 1982, 16.
24 White 1969.
25 Oxford, Ashmolean Museum, Inv. 1927.4065; ARV^2 62, 77; Vickers 1978, Figs 27–8; Boardman 1982, 15.
26 cf. Xenophon, *Symposium* 9.
27 Plutarch, *On the Glory of Athens* 3.
28 Stanford 1980, 99.
29 Hughes 1980, 367.
30 Pausanias 9.2.4.
31 ibid.

32 Plutarch, *Aristeides* 21.
33 Pausanias 10.16.3.
34 Pausanias 9.4.1.
35 Plutarch, *Aristeides* 20.
36 On Polygnotus, see Löwy 1929; Meiggs 1973, 275–7, 573.
37 Welcker 1836.
38 Plutarch, *Theseus* 29.3; cf. Davie 1982, 27.
39 Munich, Museum antiker Kleinkunst, Inv. 2640; ARV^2 402, 22.
40 Pausanias 4.2.3.
41 Such are the views of Ross Holloway 1967, esp. 100; 1973, esp. 92.
42 Bosanquet 1914, 173; cf. Glover 1945, 160–81.
43 Dawe 1967.
44 ibid., 99.
45 Francis 1983, esp.97–100.
46 *Odyssey* 8.227.
47 *Odyssey* 21.91.
48 *Odyssey* 21.94–5.
49 *Odyssey* 21.99–100.
50 *Odyssey* 2.97–8.
51 *Odyssey* 24.131–7.
52 *Odyssey* 2.97–8.
53 *Odyssey* 22.5.
54 *Odyssey* 22.27.
55 *Odyssey* 22.6–7.
56 *Odyssey* 8.140 ff.
57 *Odyssey* 8.215–22.
58 *Odyssey* 15.223–56.
59 *Odyssey* 15.525–8.
60 *Odyssey* 15.531–4. Compare the similar omens of the eagle whose augury is interpreted by Halitherses in *Odyssey* 2.146–76 and Helen in 15.160–81.
61 *Odyssey* 21.413–15.
62 cf. *Odyssey* 15.525 and Thompson 1936, 144–5 (s.v. *kirkos*). Note also that Odysseus' Phaeacian escort sped across the ocean 'faster than a hawk' (*Odyssey* 12.36).
63 *Iliad* 23.850–8. As he prepares to fight Hector who awaits his foe like a coiled snake, Achilles is compared to a hawk swooping down upon his prey (*Iliad* 22.139–44; cf. 22.93–7 and 18.485 ff.).
64 *Odyssey* 22.468–73.
65 *Odyssey* 22.474–7.
66 *Odyssey* 9.158.
67 *Odyssey* 9.159–60.
68 cf. Allen 1939, esp n. 33; Bassett 1918.
69 *Odyssey* 9.275.

70 *Odyssey* 21.259–60.
71 *Odyssey* 21.268.
72 *Odyssey* 21.278–82.
73 *Odyssey* 8.228.
74 *Odyssey* 20.345.
75 *Odyssey* 20.351–7.
76 *Odyssey* 21.3–4.
77 *Odyssey* 21.298.
78 Francis 1983, 78–9, 103–6.
79 *Odyssey* 11.6l.
80 *Odyssey* 21.296–7,301–2.
81 *Odyssey* 21.303.
82 *Odyssey* 21.304.
83 *Odyssey* 22.8–20.
84 Ashmole and Yalouris 1967, 17.
85 Robertson 1975, 283.
86 Robertson 1975, 277; Stewart 1982.
87 Lines 25–48, esp. 28 and 39.
88 Mahaffy 1876, 270.
89 Benndorf and Niemann 1890; Eichler 1950; cf. Thompson 1966, 42, n. 8; Barron 1972, 22.
90 Plutarch, *Theseus* 29; Jeffery 1965, 51.
91 Herodotus 9.27.
92 Siewert 1977, 103.
93 Pindar, *Pythian* 3.7–14.
94 Bowra 1964, 106; cf. Francis 1980, 71, n. 94.
95 Aeschines 3.186.
96 Pausanias 1.15.4.
97 Robertson 1981, 106.
98 Himerius, *Oration* 10.2.3.
99 Synesius, *Epist.* 125; ibid., 54.
100 Pausanias 1.15.3.
101 Pausanias 1.15.2.
102 Pausanias 1.15.3.
103 Pausanias 1.15.2.
104 Andrewes 1975, 9.
105 For references, see Francis and Vickers 1985a, 105, n. 2; 1985b, 99, n. 4.
106 Wycherley 1978, 40.
107 ibid., 38.
108 cf. Jeffery 1965, 50; Andrewes 1975, 13–14.
109 Francis and Vickers 1985a, 1985b, 1985c.
110 Harrison 1966.
111 Kroll 1982.

112 Athens, Agora, Inv. T 3577: Harrison 1966, pl. 37b.
113 This is the phraseology of the epigrams which reportedly accompanied the Paintings in the Stoa Poikile; see further, Francis and Vickers 1985c.
114 cf. Barron 1980, 8, n. 54: 'The equation of Trojans with Persians is a commonplace of fifth–century Athenian art'.
115 Plutarch, *Aristeides* 5.
116 Plutarch, *Cimon* 13.
117 Aeschines 3.184–5; cf. Barron 1980, 4, 8, n. 54.
118 Francis and Vickers 1985c.
119 Shear quoted by Catling 1981–2, 7.
120 cf. the significant orientation of the Altar of the Twelve Gods (Francis and Vickers 1981, 120) and, on the Athenian Treasury at Delphi, see pp. 100–4.
121 Spender 1924, 12.

5 TROPHIES FOR THE GODS

1 It is something of a topos in Athenian vase–painting, too, to show battles at the point of crisis: e.g. Figs 15–16, 18.
2 Gomme 1952, 77, 82; 1962, 29, 34.
3 Francis and Vickers 1985b, 109–13.
4 Boardman 1982, 4; contrast Habicht 1984 and 1985, esp. p. 165.
5 Pausanias 1.32.5.
6 Overbeck 1868, 200–201, 206, 210–11; Harrison 1972, 370–8.
7 Pindar, *Olympian* 9.89; 13.110; *Pythian* 8.79. On Heracles' cults, see Woodford 1971.
8 Pausanias 1.15.4.
9 Plutarch, *Theseus* 35.
10 Carne–Ross 1975, 167, citing Young 1968, 42.
11 Harrison 1966.
12 On the idealization of Marathon in the rhetorical tradition, see Loraux 1973 and 1981, 156–73.
13 Wycherley 1978, 41.
14 Tomlinson 1980.
15 Pausanias 10.25–32.
16 Pausanias 10.26.2.
17 Barron 1980, 4.
18 Wells 1923, 137.
19 ibid.
20 Pausanias 10.25.1.
21 Griffin 1980.
22 *Odyssey* 11, 367.

23 cf. the mixture of myth and banquet at the Oschophoria, Parke 1977, 78.
24 Simonides 22b, Page.
25 Simonides 531, Page.
26 Nilsson 1953, 747.
27 Aeschylus, *Eumenides* 13.
28 Pindar, *Pythian* 6.1–18.
29 Ashmole 1972, 6–8.
30 Pindar, *Olympian* 6.1–4.
31 Gardiner 1910, 119.
32 cf. *Olympian* 13.21–2 (464 BC); fr. 52i.68–70 Snell–Maehler.
33 Ashmole 1972, 6.
34 Boardman 1982, 3.
35 ibid.
36 Pausanias 10, 11, 4; cf. Boardman 1982, 4.
37 Beazley and Ashmole 1932, 27–8; Robertson 1975, 169; Ridgway 1977, 212, 217.
38 Büsing 1978; apparently misunderstood by Boardman 1982, 4, n. 13.
39 Pausanias 10.10.1.
40 Beazley and Ashmole 1932, 27–8.
41 Boardman 1982, 5.
42 For illustrations, see de La Coste Messelière 1957.
43 Boardman, 1978a, 159.
44 Boardman 1972; 1975; 1978b.
45 Boardman 1978a, 159; 1978b.
46 Woodford 1971.
47 cf. Nilsson 1951, 53.
48 cf. the recent case of Megacles and Pindar, *Pythian* 7.
49 Herodotus 2.7.1; Wycherley 1978, 33.
50 Francis and Vickers 1981, 120.
51 Pindar, *Pythian* 1.72–80.
52 Ridgway 1977, 214.
53 Herodotus 9.122.
54 Rawlinson 1875, 4, 466, n.6.
55 Gombrich 1969, 6–14.
56 ibid., 9.
57 ibid., 24.
58 ibid., 25.
59 ibid., 39.
60 Stanford 1980, 2.
61 Gombrich 1967, 46–7.
62 Lloyd–Jones 1982, x.
63 Boeckh 1811–21.

64 Wilamowitz 1982, 126.
65 ibid., 127.
66 Maittaire 1706.
67 Lloyd–Jones 1982, x.
68 Beloch 1912–27 [1893–1904], 10.
69 Fraenkel 1950, 50–1.
70 Lloyd–Jones 1982, x–xi.
71 Lloyd–Jones 1982, xi.
72 Winckelmann 1767, 86; cf. Vickers 1985, 2.
73 E. Gardner 1915, 10.
74 Thucydides 1.89.
75 Ross 1863, 30–1.
76 Ross 1855, 1, 140 and pl. 10.
77 Wilamowitz 1982, 126.
78 Ross 1855, 1, pl. 9, top; Thanks are due to Donald Bailey for advice concerning this lamp.
79 Ross 1855, 1, pl. 9, bottom. W.B. Dinsmoor believed that this skyphos was made 'around 500', and used it as evidence for dating the immediate predecessor of the Parthenon to before the Persian sack (Dinsmoor 1934, 420); J.D. Beazley, however, did not share Dinsmoor's view of the antiquity of this vessel; in fact, he doubted 'if it can be pre-Persian as is claimed' (ARV² 982).
80 Studniczska 1887.
81 cf. Furtwängler and Reichold 1904, 29.
82 The Soros at Marathon continues to be regarded as one of the major 'fixed points' in Attic chronology, but in view of the ambiguous nature of the evidence, it is difficult to understand why this should be so. When the pottery from the tomb (published in Stais 1893, and K.A. Rhomaios 1930, pls 10–14) is considered in terms of the dates conventionally ascribed to it, a curiously discrepant picture emerges. This pottery ranges from a black-figured amphora attributed to Sophilos, usually dated to 'c. 575' to numerous black-figured lekythoi thought to belong to the period of the battle of Marathon. An Attic lekane was found along with the Sophilan amphora; both vases are decorated with animals in 'Corinthianizing' fashion and have been similarly dated. Then from the 'mid-sixth century' we have a tripod pyxis decorated with scenes of Poseidon, Athena and Apollo. Another pyxis, perhaps of Euboean manufacture, contains the cremated bones of a man (whom K.A. Rhomaios optimistically identified as those of one of the Athenian generals Callimachus or Stesilaus) (Rhomaios 1930, 7). The rest of the pottery consists of a black-figure hydria, and a fragmentary red-figure cup ('c. 500'). While it is theoretically possible that the Marathon dead were honoured with very old pots, it is more likely

that the earlier vases (the amphora, lekane, and two pyxides) date from a later period than is customarily supposed while the later ones were dedicated at a time when, under Cimon, Marathon became the fuel of political propaganda. The paintings in the Stoa Poikile were one facet of this renewed interest; the construction of a large commemorative tumulus after a period of some years another. V. Stais' excavations provided evidence of small–scale votary activity (Stais 1893, 50–3). Herodotus' report of the tomb of the Aeginetans at Plataea (9.85.3), 'made ten years later' than the battle, provides a parallel – and perhaps the occasion – for possible Cimonian refurbishment at Marathon. To confuse complicated issues even further, S. Koumanoudes has recently argued that the Soros at Marathon may not even be the grave of the Marathonian dead (Koumanoudes 1978). If he is correct, then those who accept his arguments can obviously no longer regard the monument as a 'fixed point'.

83 Studniczska 1887, 159.
84 cf. Vickers 1985, 22–3.
85 Francis and Vickers 1981, 97.
86 A notable exception: Emmanuel Löwy (Löwy 1937, 1938).

APPENDIX: THE MOTHER, THE DEMOS, AND THE DEMOSION

1 A lecture given on 12 April 1985 at a meeting of the Classical Association of the Middle West and South.
2 Fraenkel 1942, 249.
3 e.g. Kahrstedt 1938; Hignett 1952, 14–15; Harrison 1955; Bradeen 1963, 205, n. 88; Stroud 1968, 28–9; Boegehold 1972, 28–30.
4 Thompson 1937, 140.
5 Picard 1938.
6 Boersma 1970, 31–2.
7 Thompson 1937, 222; 1982, 136–7; cf. Francis and Vickers 1988.
8 Pindar, *Pythian* 3, 78; fr. 80 (Snell).
9 Pausanias 3, 22, 4.
10 But see now de la Genière 1985, 1986.
11 Chantraine 1966.
12 Nilsson 1941, 687, n. 3.
13 Thompson and Wycherley 1972, 31.
14 Wycherley 1978, 35.
15 Guthrie 1954, 188; Burkert 1985, 178.
16 Haldane 1968, 19.
17 Stevens 1954.

18 Thompson 1937, 195.
19 Thompson and Wycherley 1972, 31.
20 Aeschines 3.187.
21 Pausanias 1.3.5.
22 ibid.; cf. Arrian, *Periplus* 19.
23 Pliny, *Natural History* 36.17.
24 Carpenter 1960, 153.
25 Thompson and Wycherley 1972, 31.
26 Posner 1972, 103.
27 Thompson and Wycherley 1972, 38; cf. Thompson 1937, 217.
28 Ferguson 1944, 1949; Dodds 1951, 193–4.
29 Stroud 1978, 40, n. 43.
30 Boegehold 1972, 29.
31 Schwyzer 1923, no. 409.
32 Dörpfeld 1935, 1, 99.
33 I thank J.H. Kroll for discussing this suggestion with me.
34 Boegehold 1972, 29.
35 Thompson 1982, 136, n. 11.
36 *FGH* 72 F 13.
37 Thompson 1981, 346.
38 Thompson 1978, 1981, 1982.
39 Thompson 1982, 136.
40 Jacoby 1949, 383–4.
41 [Hippocrates] *Sacred Disease* 4.20.

ABBREVIATIONS

AA	*Archäologischer Anzeiger*
AAA	*Athens Annals of Archaeology*
ABV	J.D. Beazley, *Attic Black–figure Vase–painters*, Oxford 1956
AJA	*American Journal of Archaeology*
ARV²	J.D. Beazley, *Attic Red–figure Vase–painters*, Oxford 1963
BCH	*Bulletin de Correspondance Hellénique*
BICS	*Bulletin of the Institute of Classical Studies*
BSA	*Annual of the British School at Athens*
CR	*Classical Review*
CRAI	*Comptes–rendues de l'Académie des Inscriptions et Belles-Lettres*
CSCA	*California Studies in Classical Antiquity*
FGH	F. Jacoby, *Fragmente der griechischen Historiker*, 1923–
GRBS	*Greek, Roman and Byzantine Studies*
HSCP	*Harvard Studies in Classical Philology*
HTR	*Harvard Theological Review*
IG	*Inscriptiones Graecae*
JdI	*Jarbuch des deutschen archäologischen Instituts*
JHS	*Journal of Hellenic Studies*
JRS	*Journal of Roman Studies*
LSJ	H.G. Liddell, R. Scott, and H.S. Jones, *A Greek-English Lexicon*, 9th edn, Oxford, 1940
MEFRA	*Mélanges de l'École Française à Rome: Antiquité*
Para.	J.D. Beazley, *Paralipomena*, Oxford, 1971
PBA	*Proceedings of the British Academy*
PCPS	*Proceedings of the Cambridge Philological Society*

RA	*Revue archéologique*
REA	*Revue des Études anciennes*
SbBayern	*Sitzungsberichte der königlichen Bayerischen Akademie der Wissenschaften, Philosophisch–philologische Classe*
SbWien	*Sitzungsbericht der Akademie der Wissenschaften in Wien*
Studies Thompson	*Studies in Athenian Architecture, Sculpture and Topography presented to Homer A. Thompson, Hesperia,* Suppl. 20, 1982
TAPA	*Transactions of the American Philological Association*
ZPE	*Zeitschrift für Papyrologie und Epigraphik*

BIBLIOGRAPHY

Agora Guide (1954), *The Athenian Agora: A Guide to the Excavations*, Athens.

Agora Guide (1962), *The Athenian Agora: A Guide*, Athens.

Åkerström, (1943), *Der geometrische Stil in Italien. Archäologische Grundlagen der frühesten historischen Zeit Italiens*, Lund/Leipzig.

Allen, W. (1939), 'The theme of the suitors in the *Odyssey*', *TAPA* 70, 104–24.

Andrewes, A. (1975), 'Could there have been a battle at Oenoe?', in Levick 1975, 9–16.

Ashmole, B. (1972), *Architect and Sculptor in Classical Greece*, New York.

Ashmole, B., Yalouris, N. and Frantz, A. (1967), *Olympia, the Sculpture of the Temple of Zeus*, London.

Athens Comes of Age: From Solon to Salamis, Papers of a symposium sponsored by the Archaeological Institute of America, Princeton Society and the Department of Art and Archaeology, Princeton University, Princeton, NJ.

Auberson, P. (1968), *Eretria* 1, Bern.

Auberson, P. and Schefold, K. (1972), *Führer durch Eretria*, Bern.

Bacon, H. (1961), *Barbarians in Greek Tragedy*, New Haven, Conn.

Bapp, K. (1921), *Aus Goethes griechischer Gedankenwelt*, Leipzig.

Barrett, W.S. (1964), *Euripides: Hippolytus*, Oxford.

Barron, J.P. (1972), 'New light on old walls', *JHS* 92, 20–45.

Barron, J.P. (1980), 'Bakchylides, Theseus and a woolly cloak', *BICS* 27, 1–8.

Bassett, S.E. (1918), 'The suitors of Penelope', *TAPA* 49, 42–4.

Beazley, J.D. and Ashmole, B. (1932), *Greek Sculpture and Painting*, Cambridge.

Beloch, K.J. (1912–27), *Griechische Geschichte*, 2nd edn [1st edn 1893–1904], Strasburg.

Benndorf, O. and Niemann, G. (1890), *Das Heroon von Gjölbaschi-Trysa*, Vienna.

Bérard, C. (1987), *Actes du Colloque international 'Images et sociétés en Grèce ancienne: l'iconographie comme méthode d'analyse', Lausanne, 1984*, Lausanne.

Boardman, J. (1972), 'Herakles, Peisistratos and sons', *RA*, 57–72.

Boardman, J. (1975), 'Herakles, Peisistratos and Eleusis', *JHS* 95, 1–12.

Boardman, J. (1978a), *Greek Sculpture: The Archaic Period*, London.

Boardman, J. (1978b), 'Herakles, Delphi and Kleisthenes of Sikyon', *RA*, 227–34.

Boardman, J. (1982), 'Herakles, Theseus and Amazons', in Kurtz and Sparkes 1982, 1–28.

Boardman, J. (1984), '*Signa tabulae priscae artis*', *JHS* 104, 161–3.

Boeckh, A. (1811–21), *Pindari Opera*, Berlin.

Boegehold, A.L. (1972), 'The establishment of a central archive at Athens', *AJA* 76, 23–30.

Boersma, J.S. (1970), *Athenian Building Policy from 561/0 to 405/4 BC* (Scripta Archaeologica Groningana, 4), Groningen.

Boettiger, K.A. (ed.) (1820–5), *Amalthea*, Leipzig.

Bosanquet, E.S. (1914), *Days in Attica*, London.

Bothmer, D. von (1970), 'Greek and Roman art', *Bulletin of the Metropolitan Museum* 29, 82–3.

Bowra, C.M. (1964), *Pindar*, Oxford.

Bradeen, D.W. (1963), 'The fifth century archon list', *Hesperia* 32, 187–208.

Brommer, F. (1982), *Theseus: die Taten des griechischen Helden in der antiken Kunst und Literatur*, Darmstadt.

Broneer, O. (1944), 'The tent of Xerxes and the Greek theater', *University of California Publications in Classical Archaeology* 1 (1944), 305–11.

Broneer, O. (1952), 'Odeion and skene', *AJA* 56, 172.

Brunn, H. (1881), 'Exegetische Beiträge 2. Die Dareiosvase', *SbBayern*, 103–8.

Brunnsåker, S. (1971), *The Tyrant-slayers of Kritios and Nesiotes*, 2nd edn, Stockholm.

Burkert, W. (1985), *Greek Religion: Archaic and Classical*, Oxford.

Burn, A.R. (1977), 'Thermopylai revisited and some topographical notes on Marathon and Plataiai', in Kinzl (ed.) 1977, 90–105.

Burn, A.R. (1984), *Persia and the Greeks: The Defence of the West 546–478 B.C.*, 2nd edn, London.

Burnett, A.P. (1984), *The Art of Bacchylides*, Cambridge, Mass.

Büsing, H.H. (1978), 'Ein Anthemion in Delphi', in Kopcke and Moore 1978, 29–36.

Carne–Ross, D.S. (1975), 'Three preludes for Pindar', *Arion* 2, 160–9.

Carpenter, R. (1960), *Greek Sculpture*, Chicago.

Catling, H.W. (1981–2), 'Archaeology in Greece 1981–82', in *Archaeological Reports* 28, 3–62.

Chantraine, P. (1966), 'Questions de syntaxe grecque: 1 Encore *en agras*', *Revue de Philologie*, 3rd series, 40, 37–9.

Cook, J.M. (1983), *The Persian Empire*, London.

Cornford, F.M. (1907), *Thucydides Mythistoricus*, London.

Coulton, J.J. (1977), *Greek Architects at Work*, London.

Coulton, J.J. (1979), 'Doric capitals: a proportional analysis', *BSA* 74, 81–153.

Davie, J.N. (1982), 'Theseus the king in fifth century Athens', *Greece and Rome*, 2nd series, 25–34.

Davies, J.K. (1971), *Athenian Propertied Families, 600–300 B.C.*, Oxford.

Davies, M. (1981), 'Artemon transvestitus', *Mnemosyne* 34, 288–99.

Dawe, R.D. (1967), 'Reflections on *Ate* and *Hamartia*', *HSCP* 72, 89–123.

Devambez, P. (1976), 'Le Groupe statuaire des Amazones à Éphèse', *CRAI*, 162–70.

Dinsmoor, W.B. (1934), 'The date of the older Parthenon', *AJA* 37, 408–48.

Dodds, E.R. (1951), *The Greeks and the Irrational*, Berkeley, Calif.

Doumas, C. (1963), 'Kea', *Archailogikon Deltion* 18/2, 281–2.

Dover, K.J. (1978), *Greek Homosexuality*, London.

Dunbabin, T.J. (1949), Review of Åkerström 1943, *JRS* 39, 137–41.

Edwards, M.W. (1978), 'Agamemnon's decision: freedom and folly in Aeschylus', *CSCA* 10, 17–38.

Ehrenberg, V. (1973), *From Solon to Socrates*, 2nd edn, London.

Eichler, F. (1950), *Die Reliefs des Heroon von Gjölbaschi–Trysa*, Vienna.

Fagles, R., Bowra, C.M., and Parry, A.M. (1961), *Bacchylides: Complete Poems*, New Haven, Conn.

Ferguson, W.S. (1944), 'The Attic Orgeones', *HTR* 37, 61–140.

Ferguson, W.S. (1949), 'Orgeonika', in *Commemorative Studies in Honor of Theodore Leslie Shear*, Princeton, NJ.

Finley, J.H., Jr (1966), 'Politics and early Attic tragedy', *HSCP* 71, 1–14.

Fraenkel, E. (1942), 'Aeschylus: new texts and old problems', *PBA* 28, 237–58.

Fraenkel, E. (ed.) (1950), *Aeschylus Agamemnon*, Oxford.

Francis, E.D. (1975), 'Menandrian maids and Mithraic lions', *Glotta* 53, 43–66.

Francis, E.D. (1980), 'Greeks and Persians: the art of hazard and triumph', in D. Schmandt–Besserat (ed.), *Ancient Persia: the Art of an Empire*, Malibu, Calif., 53–86.

Francis, E.D. (1983), 'Virtue, folly, and Greek etymology', in Rubino and Shelmerdine 1983, 74–121.

Francis, E.D. and Vickers, M. (1981), 'Leagros kalos', *PCPS* n.s. 27, 97–136.

Francis, E.D. and Vickers, M. (1983), 'Signa priscae artis: Eretria and Siphnos', JHS 103, 49–67.

Francis, E.D. and Vickers, M. (1984), Review of Brommer 1982, JHS 104, 267–8.

Francis, E.D. and Vickers, M. (1985a), 'Argive Oenoe', L'Antiquité Classique 54, 105–15.

Francis, E.D. and Vickers, M. (1985b), 'The Oenoe painting in the Stoa Poikile, and Herodotus' account of Marathon', BSA 80, 99–111.

Francis, E.D. and Vickers, M. (1985c), 'The Marathon epigram in the Stoa Poikile', Mnemosyne 38, 390–3.

Francis, E.D. and Vickers, M. (1988), 'The Agora revisited; Athenian chronology c. 500–450 B.C.', BSA 83.

Frazer, J. (1898), Pausanias' Description of Greece, London.

Fries, C. (1903), 'Babylonische Feuerpost', Klio 3, 169–70.

Fries, C. (1904), 'Zur Babylonischen Feuerpost', Klio 4, 117–21.

Frisk, H.J. (1954–72), Griechisches etymologisches Wörterbuch, Heidelberg.

Furtwängler, A. and Reichold, K. (1904), Griechische Vasenmalerei 1, Munich.

Gall, H. von (1977), 'Das persische Königszelt und die Hallenarchitektur in Iran und Griechenland', in Höckmann and Krug 1977, 119–32.

Gall, H. von (1979), 'Das Zelt des Xerxes und seine Rolle als persicher Raumtyp in Griechenland', Gymnasion 86, 444–62.

Gardiner, E.N. (1910), Greek Athletic Sports and Festivals, London.

Gardner, E. (1915), A Handbook of Greek Sculpture, 2nd edn, London.

Gardner, P. (1926), New Chapters in Greek Art, Oxford.

Gauer, W. (1968), Weihgeschenke aus den Perserkriegen (Istanbuler Mitteilungen 2), Tübingen.

Gauer, W. (1980), 'Das Athener Schatzhaus und die marathonischen Akrothinia in Delphi', in Krinzinger et al. 1980, 127–36.

Genière, J. de la (1986), 'De la Phrygie à Locres Épizéphyrienne: les chemins de Cybèle', MEFRA 97, 693–718.

Genière, J. de la (1986), 'Le Culte de la Mère des dieux dans le Péloponnèse', CRAI, 29–48.

Gill, D.W.J. (1988), 'The Temple of Apahaia on Aegina: the date of the reconstruction', BSA 83.

Glover, T.R. (1945), Springs of Hellas and other Essays, Cambridge.

Gombrich, E.H. (1969), In Search of Cultural History (The Philip Maurice Deneke Lecture 1967), Oxford.

Gomme, A.W. (1952), 'Herodotus and Marathon', Phoenix 6, 75–83.

Gomme, A.W. (1962), More Essays in Greek History and Literature, Oxford.

Griffin, J. (1980), Homer on Life and Death, Oxford.

Griffin, J. (1983a), Review of Macleod 1982, CR 33, 1–5.

Griffin, J. (1983b), Review of Veyne 1983, *TLS* 22 April, 398.

Guthrie, W.K.C. (1954), *The Greeks and their Gods*, Boston.

Habicht, C. (1984), 'Pausanias and the evidence of inscriptions', *Classical Antiquity* 3, 40–56.

Habicht, C. (1985), *Pausanias' Guide to Ancient Greece*, Berkeley, Calif.

Haldane, J. (1968), 'Pindar and Pan: frs 95–100 Snell', *Phoenix* 22, 18–31.

Hammond, N.G.L. (1982), 'The narrative of Herodotus vii and the decree of Themistocles at Troezen', *JHS* 102, 75–93.

Harrison, A.R.W. (1955), 'Law-making at Athens at the end of the fifth century B.C.', *JHS* 75, 26–35.

Harrison, E.B. (1965), *Archaic and Archaistic Sculpture* (The Athenian Agora 11), Princeton, NJ.

Harrison, E.B. (1966), 'The composition of the Amazonomachy on the shield of Athena Parthenos', *Hesperia* 35, 107–33.

Harrison, E.B. (1972), 'The south frieze of the Nike temple and the Marathon painting in the Stoa Poikile', *AJA* 76, 353–78.

Helbig, W. (1966), *Führer durch die öffentlichen Sammlungen klassischer Altertümer in Rom*, 3rd edn, Tübingen.

Hignett, C. (1952), *A History of the Athenian Constitution to the end of the Fifth Century B.C.*, Oxford.

Hinks, R. (1939), *Myth and Allegory in Ancient Art*, London.

Höckmann, U. and Krug, A. (1977), *Festschrift für Frank Brommer*, Mainz.

Hoffmann, H. (1961), 'The Persian origin of Attic rhyta', *Antike Kunst* 4, 21–6.

Hölscher, F. (1973), *Griechische Historienbilder*, 30–1, 233, nn.62–6.

Hornbostel, W.B. (1982), 'Erwerbungen für die Antikenabteilung in den Jahren 1980–81', *Jahrbuch des Museums für Kunst und Gewerbe Hamburg* n.s. 1, 101–26.

Hughes, R. (1980), *The Shock of the New*, London.

Huxley, G.L. (1973), 'The date of Pherekydes of Athens', *GRBS* 14, 137–43.

Huxley, G.L. (1978), 'Simonides and his world', *Proceedings of the Royal Irish Academy* 78, C, 9, 231–47.

Jacoby, F. (1949), *Atthis: the Local Chronicles of Ancient Athens*, Oxford.

Jameson, M. (1962), 'A revised text of the decree of Themistocles from Troizen', *Hesperia* 31, 310–15.

Jebb, R.C. (1882), 'Pindar', *JHS* 3, 144–83.

Jebb, R.C. (1905), *Bacchylides, the Poems and Fragments*, Cambridge.

Jeffery, L.H. (1965), 'The *Battle of Oinoe* in the Stoa Poikile: a problem in Greek art and history', *BSA* 60, 41–57.

Kahrstedt, U. (1938), 'Untersuchungen zur athenische Behördern', *Klio* 31, 25–32.

143

Kenyon, F.G. (1897), *The Poems of Bacchylides*, London.

Kinzl, K.H. (ed.) (1977), *Greece and the Eastern Mediterranean in Ancient History and Prehistory*, Berlin.

Kinzl, K.H. (1978), '*Demokratia*: Studie zur Frühgeschichte des Begriffes', *Gymnasium* 85, 117–27, 312–26.

Kirk, G.T. (1954), Review of Wade–Gery 1952, *JHS* 74, 190–1.

Kopcke, G. and Moore, M. (1978), *Studies in Classical Art and Archaeology: A Tribute to P.H. Blanckenhagen*, New York.

Koumanoudis, P. (1978), 'A Marathon', *AAA* 11, 232–44.

Kourouniotis, K. (1900), '*Anaskaphai en Eretriai*', *Praktika*, 53–6.

Krinzinger, F., Otto, B., and Walde–Psenner, E. (1980), *Forschungen und Funde: Festschrift für Bernhard Neutsch*, Innsbruck.

Kroll, J.H. (1982), 'The ancient image of Athena Polias', in *Studies Thompson*, 64–76.

Kurtz, D.C. and Sparkes, B.(1982), *The Eye of Greece: Studies in the Art of Athens* [Martin Robertson Festschrift], Cambridge.

La Coste Messelière, P. de (1957), *Sculptures du Trésor des Athéeniens* (*Fouilles de Delphes* 4, 4), Paris.

Langlotz, E. (1920), *Zeitbestimmung der strengrotfiguren Vasenmalerei und der gleichzeitigen Plastik*, Leipzig.

Latte, K. (1968), *Kleine Schriften zur Religion, Recht, Literatur und Sprache der Griechen und Römern*, Munich.

Letronne, M. (1836), *Lettres d'un antiquaire à un artiste sur l'emploi de la peinture historique murale dans la décoration des temples et des autres édifices publics ou particuliers chez les Grecs et les Romains*, Paris.

Levick, B. (ed.) (1975), *The Ancient Historian and his Materials: Essays in Honour of C.E. Stevens on his Birthday*, Farnborough, Hants.

Lewis, D.M. (1977), *Sparta and Persia* (Cincinnati Classical Studies, n.s. 1), Leiden.

Lloyd–Jones, H. (1982), 'Introduction', in Wilamowitz–Moellendorff 1982, v–xxxii.

Loraux, N. (1981), '"Marathon" ou l'histoire idéologique', *REA* 75, 13–42.

Loraux, N. (1981), *L'invention d'Athènes. Histoire de l'oraison funèbre dans la "cité classique"*, Paris.

Löwy, E. (1929), *Polygnot, ein Buch von griechischer Malerei*, Vienna.

Löwy, E. (1937), 'Zur Datierung attischer Inschriften', *SbWien* 206/4.

Löwy, E. (1938), 'Der Beginn der rotfigurigen Vasenmalerei', *SbWien* 207/2.

MacDowell, D.M. (1960), 'Aigina and the Delian League', *JHS* 80, 118–21.

Macleod, C.W. (1982), *Homer, Iliad Book 24*, Cambridge.

Macleod, C.W. (1982), 'Politics and the *Oresteia*', *JHS* 102, 124–44.

Mahaffy, J.H. (1876), *Rambles and Studies in Greece*, London.

Maittaire, M. (1706), *Graecae linguae Dialecti*, London.

Mallwitz, A. (1972), *Olympia und seine Bauten*, Munich.

Meiggs, R. (1973), *The Athenian Empire*, corrected reprint, Oxford.

Meritt, B.D., Wade–Gery, H.T., and McGregor, M.F. (1939–53), *The Athenian Tribute Lists*, Cambridge, Mass.

Merkelbach, R. (1973), 'Der Theseus des Bakchylides (Gedicht für ein attisches Ephebenfest)', *ZPE* 12, 56–72.

Mitten, D.G., Pedley, J., and Scott, J.A. (eds) (1971), *Studies Presented to George M. Hanfmann*, Mainz.

Murray, G. (1946), 'The future of Greek studies', *JHS* 65, 1–9.

Murray, O. (1990), *Sympotica*, Oxford.

Mylonas, G. and Raymond, D. (eds) (1953), *Studies Presented to D.M. Robinson* 2, St Louis, Mo.

Myres, J.L. (1953), *Herodotus: Father of History*, Oxford.

Nagy, G. (1973), 'Phaethon, Sappho's Phaon, and the white rock of Leucas', *HSCP* 77, 137–77.

Nilsson, M. (1941), *Geschichte der griechischen Religion* 1, Munich.

Nilsson, M. (1951), *Cults, Myths, Oracles and Politics in Ancient Greece*, Lund.

Nilsson, M. (1953), 'Political propaganda in sixth century Athens', in Mylonas and Raymond 1953.

Nylander, C. (1970), *Ionians in Pasargadae: Studies in Old Persian Architecture*, Uppsala.

Ostby, E. (1980), 'The Athenaion of Karthaia', *Opuscula Atheniensia* 13, 189–223.

Overbeck, J. (1868), *Die antiken Schriftquellen zur Geschichte der bildenden Künste bei den Griechen*, Leipzig.

Parke, H.W. (1977), *Festivals of the Athenians*, London.

Picard, C. (1938) 'Le Complexe Métroon–Bouleuterion–Prytanikon, à l'Agora d'Athènes', *RA* 6th series, 12, 97–101.

Podlecki, A.J. (1971), 'Cimon, Skyros and "Theseus' bones"', *JHS* 91, 141–3.

Posner, E. (1972), *Archives in the Ancient World*, Cambridge, Mass.

Quincey, J.H. (1963), 'The beacon–sites in the *Agamemnon*', *JHS* 83, 118–32.

Ras, S. (1944–5), 'L'Amazonomachie du bouclier de l'Athéna Parthénos', *BCH* 68–9, 163–205.

Raubitschek, A.E. (1955), 'Menon, son of Menekleides', *Hesperia* 24, 286–9.

Rawlinson, G. (1875), *History of Herodotus*, 3rd edn, London.

Redfield, J.M. (1975), *Nature and Culture in the Iliad: the Tragedy of Hector*, Chicago.

Rhodes, P.J. (1972), *The Athenian Boule*, Oxford; reprinted with appendix 1982.

Rhodes, P.J. (1981), *A Commentary on the Aristotelian* Athenaion Politeia, Oxford.

Rhomaios, K.A. (1930), *Corpus Vasorum Antiquorum: Athens*, Paris.

Ridgway, B.S. (1974), 'A story of five Amazons', *AJA* 78, 1–17.

Ridgway, B.S. (1977), *The Archaic Style in Greek Sculpture*, Princeton, NJ.

Robert, C. (1898), 'Theseus und Meleagros bei Bakchylides', *Hermes* 33, 132–47.

Robertson, M. (1975), *A History of Greek Art*, Cambridge.

Robertson, M. (1981), *A Shorter History of Greek Art*, Cambridge.

Ross, L. (1855), *Archäologische Aufsätze*, Leipzig.

Ross, L. (1863), *Erinnerungen und Mittheilungen aus Griechenland*, Berlin.

Ross Holloway, R. (1967), 'PanHellenism in the sculptures of the Zeus Temple at Olympia', *GRBS* 8, 93–101.

Ross Holloway, R. (1973), *A View of Greek Art*, Providence, RI.

Rubino, C.A. and Shelmerdine, C.W. (1983), *Approaches to Homer*, Austin, Tex.

Schefold, K. (1946), 'Kleisthenes. Der Anteil der Kunst an der Gestaltung des jungen attischen Freistaates', *Museum Helveticum* 3, 59–93.

Schmidt, E.F. (1939), 'The Treasury at Persepolis and other discoveries in the homeland of the Achaemenians', *Oriental Institute Communications* 21, Chicago.

Schmidt, E.F. (1953), *Persepolis*, Chicago.

Schmidt, M. (1960), *Der Dareiosmaler und sein Umkreis (Orbis Antiquus* 15), Münster.

Schwyzer, E. (1923), *Dialectorum Graecarum exempla epigraphica potiora*, Leipzig.

Segal, C.P. (1979), 'The myth of Bacchylides 17', *Eranos* 77, 23–37.

Seznec, J. (1953), *The Survival of the Pagan Gods*, Princeton, NJ.

Shapiro, H.A. (1982), 'Theseus, Athens and Troizen', *AA*, 291–7.

Shear, T.L., Jr (1978), 'Tyrants and buildings in Archaic Athens' in *Athens Comes of Age*.

Shear, T.L., Jr (1981), 'Discovery of the Painted Stoa and other classical monuments in the Athenian Agora', *American School of Classical Studies Newsletter* (Fall), 4–5.

Siewert, P. (1977), 'The ephebic oath in fifth century Athens', *JHS* 97, 102–11.

Sourvinou–Inwood, C. (1971), 'Theseus lifting the rock and a cup near the Pithos Painter', *JHS* 91, 94–100.

Sourvinou–Inwood, C. (1979), *Theseus as Son and Stepson*, *BICS*, Suppl. 40.

Spender, H. (1924), *Byron and Greece*, London.

Stais, V. (1893), 'Ho en Marathoni tymbos', *Athenische Mitteilungen* 18, 46–63, pls 2–5.

Stanford, W.B. (1980), *The Enemies of Poetry*, London.

Stevens, G.P. (1954), 'Lintel with painted lioness', *Hesperia* 23, 169–84.

Stewart, A.F. (1979), *Attika: Studies in Athenian Sculpture of the Hellenistic Age*, Society for the Promotion of Hellenic Studies, Supplementary Paper 14.

Stewart, A.F. (1982), 'Pindaric *dike* and the Temple of Zeus at Olympia', *Classical Antiquity* 2, 133–44.

Stroud, R.S. (1968), *Drakon's Law on Homicide*, University of California Publications, Classical Studies 3.

Stroud, R.S. (1978), 'State documents in archaic Athens', in *Athens Comes of Age*.

Studniczska, F. (1887), 'Antenor der Sohn des Eumares und die Geschichte der archaischen Malerei iv. Zur Zeitbestimmung der Vasenmalerei mit roten Figuren', *Jdl* 2, 159–68.

Thompson, D.B. (1956), 'The Persian spoils in Athens', in Weinberg 1956, 281–91.

Thompson, D'A. W. (1936), *A Glossary of Greek Birds*, London and Oxford.

Thompson, H.A. (1937), 'Buildings on the west side of the Agora', *Hesperia* 6, 1–226.

Thompson, H.A. (1940), 'The Tholos of Athens and its Predecessors', *Hesperia*, Suppl. 4.

Thompson, H.A. (1966), 'Activity in the Athenian Agora 1960–65', *Hesperia* 35, 33–54.

Thompson, H.A. (1978), Review of Wycherley 1978, *Archaeology* 31/5, 63–5.

Thompson, H.A. (1981), 'Athens faces adversity', *Hesperia* 50, 343–55.

Thompson, H.A. (1982), 'The Pnyx in models', in *Studies Vanderpool*, 133–47.

Thompson, H.A. and Wycherley, R.E. (1972), *The Agora of Athens: The History, Shape and Uses of an Ancient City Center* (The Athenian Agora 14), Princeton, NJ.

Tomlinson, R.A. (1980), 'Two notes on *hestiatoria* 2. The Lesche of the Cnidians', *BSA* 75, 224–8.

Travlos, J. (1971), *A Pictorial Dictionary of Athens*, London.

Tuchelt, K. (1962), *Tiergefässe in Kopf– und Protomengestalt. Untersuchungen zur Formgeschichte tierförmiger Giessgefässe*, Istanbuler Forschungen 22.

Vanderpool, E. (1966), 'A monument to the battle of Marathon', *Hesperia* 35, 93–106.

Veyne, P. (1983), *Les Grecs ont–ils cru à leurs mythes? Essai sur l'imagination constituante*, Paris.

Vickers, M. (1978), *Greek Vases*, Oxford.

Vickers, M. (1985a), 'Early Greek coinage, a reassessment', *Numismatic Chronicle* 145, 1–44.

Vickers, M. (1985b), 'Persepolis, Vitruvius and the Erechtheum Caryatids: the iconography of medism and servitude', *Revue archéologique*, 3–28.

Vickers, M. (1987), 'Dates, methods and icons', in Bérard 1987, 19–25.

Vickers, M. (1989), 'Alcibiades on stage: *Thesmophoriazusae* and *Helen*', *Historia* 36, 41–65.

Vickers, M. (1990), 'Athenian symposia after the Persian wars', in Murray 1990.

Vidal–Naquet, P. (1981), *Le Chasseur noir: formes de pensée et formes de société dans le monde grec*, Paris.

Wade–Gery, H.T. (1952), *The Poet of the Iliad*, Cambridge.

Walbank, F.W. (1967), *Historical Commentary on Polybius* 2, Oxford.

Walsh, J. (1986), 'The date of the Athenian stoa at Delphi' *AJA* 90, 319–36.

Waters, K.H. (1971), *Herodotus on Tyrants and Despots*, Wiesbaden.

Weinberg, S. (ed.) (1956), *The Aegean and the Near East: Studies Presented to Hetty Goldman*, Locust Valley.

Welcker, F.G. (1836), Review of Letronne 1836, *Allgemeine Litteratur Zeitung*, 145–239.

Wells, J. (1923), *Studies in Herodotus*, Oxford.

Westlake, H.D. (1936), 'The medism of Thessaly', *JHS* 36, 12–24.

White, M. (1969), 'Herodotus' starting point', *Phoenix* 23, 39–48.

Wilamowitz–Moellendorff, U. von (1937), *Kleine Schriften* 1, Berlin.

Wilamowitz–Moellendorff, U. von (1982), *History of Classical Scholarship*, London.

Williams, D. (1982), 'Aegina, Aphaia–Tempel iv. The inscription commemorating the construction of the first limestone temple and other features of the sixth century temenos', *AA*, 55–68.

Winckelmann, J.J. (1767), *Anmerkungen über die Geschichte der Kunst des Alterthums*, Dresden.

Woodford, S. (1971), 'Cults of Heracles in Attica', in Mitten, *et al*. 1971, 211–26.

Woodford, S. (1974), 'More light on old walls: the Theseus of the Centauromachy in the Theseion', *JHS* 94, 158–65.

Wycherley, R.E. (1959), 'The temple of Hephaistos', *JHS* 79, 153–6.

Wycherley, R.E. (1978), *The Stones of Athens*, Princeton, NJ.

Young, D.C. (1968), *Three Odes of Pindar*, Leiden.

Zuntz, G. (1955), *The Political Plays of Euripides*, Manchester.

INDEX OF CLASSICAL AUTHORS

Numbers in italic refer to the original sources, those in roman to the pages on which they are quoted in this book.

GENERAL INDEX

151

Athens, Acropolis 22, 49, 50, 67, 88,
109, 119; Archaic temple of Athena
22; Cave of Pan 33; Persian spoils
89; statue of Athena Promachos 74
Athens, Agora 22, 23, 85; Altar of
the Twelve Gods 103; Cultstatue of
Mother 116; Great Drain 18, 23,
113; Hellenistic Metroon 115–17;
'Metroon' 17–19, 112–15, 117,
118; New Bouleuterion 18, 115,
116; Old Bouleuterion 7–19, 22,
23, 113–19; Record Office 19, 22,
112, 116–20; Stoa Poikile 67,
85, 87, 90, 94, 97, 103, 104;
Amazonomachy 88–9, 94;
Marathon 85–7, 90–1, 93; *Oenoe* 87,
92; *Troy Taken* 86, 88,
89, 94; Temple of Apollo Patroos
17; Tholos 5, 17–19, 21, 22,
119; victory epigrams on herms 62
Athens, Agrae 113
Athens, Arch of Hadrian 66
Athens, Areopagus 53
Athens, Eridanos River 90
Athens, Odeion of Pericles 5
Athens, Pnyx 22, 23
Athens, Prytaneis 18, 21
Athens, public burial 67
Athens, Sanctuary of the Dioscuri 53
Athens, Theatre of Dionysus 5
Athens, Theseum 49, 50, 53, 55,
61, 69–70, 73, 75, 87, 97, 98,
103
Athens, water supply 23
Athos 32
Atossa 1, 5, 20, 30, 32
Attalus of Pergamum 8
Attica, olive groves 75

Babylon 33
Bacchylides 45, 50, 53–5,
57–64, 67, 69, 71, 72, 83, 84,
93, 99
Bellerophon 3, 38, 39
Bendis 118
Bent, Theodore 30
Black Sea 27, 28
Boeckh, August 106
Boges 62

Briseis Painter 60–2, 64
Brygos Painter 40, 41, 58
Burkhardt, Jakob 105–6
Byron, Lord 90
Byzantium 57

Callias Laccoplutus 89
Callimachus 88
Cambyses 34
Carpaccio, *Legend of St Ursula* 24
Carthaea, Temple of Athena 63
Carystus 12, 14
Cassandra 32, 34, 86
Centauromachy 50, 51, 69, 70,
75, 81–3, 104
Ceos 63
Chalcidice 48
Chalcis 13, 14
Chersonnese, Thracian 48
Chimaera 3, 38, 39
Cicero, *Letters to Atticus* 106
Cicones 79
Cimon 2, 14, 15, 19, 34, 46–9,
52, 53, 55–8, 62, 63, 65–70,
74, 75, 84, 86, 87, 89, 91,
94–6, 98, 102, 103, 109, 120
Cineas 70
Cithaeron 104
Cleisthenes 18, 21, 23, 24, 46,
47, 65, 112, 113, 119, 120
Cleomenes, king of Sparta 26
Clytemnestra 32–4, 36
Cnidians 95
Crete 46, 56, 60, 65
Croesus 2, 71, 72
Cumae 104
Cybele 17, 25, 112–14, 118
Cynchreus 56
Cyprus 27, 28
Cyrus the Great 2, 71, 72, 105

Darius 1, 5, 9, 12, 32, 36–8,
41, 95
Darius Painter 36, 39
Datis 100
Delian League 27, 29, 58, 62,
63, 65, 95
Delos 33, 51, 64
Delphi 73, 85, 98; Athenian

DATE DUE

GAYLORD | | | PRINTED IN U.S.A.